A Student's Guide
to Methodology

A Student's Guide to
Methodology

Justifying Enquiry

PETER CLOUGH AND
CATHY NUTBROWN

SAGE Publications
London • Thousand Oaks • New Delhi

SAGE Publications Company
6 Bonhill Street
London EC2A 4PU

SAGE Publications Inc
2455 Teller Road
Thousand Oaks, California 91320

SAGE Publications India Pvt Ltd
32, M-Block Market
Greater Kailash - I
New Delhi 110 048

Library of Congress Control Number: 2002104223

A catalogue record for this book is available from the
British Library

ISBN 0 7619 7421 0
ISBN 0 7619 7422 9 (pbk)

Typeset by Dorwyn Ltd, Hampshire
Printed in Great Britain by Athenaeum Press

Contents

Acknowledgements

This book has evolved from our many teaching interactions with Masters and PhD students in the UK and overseas and we acknowledge, with gratitude, the various roles of our students and colleagues at the University of Sheffield, UK in the shaping of some of the ideas contained here.

Specifically, we should like to thank: Wilfred Carr, Di Chilvers, Polly Dyer, Jeanette Graham, Susie Home, Peter Hannon, Barry Jackson, Marianne Lagrange, Jon Nixon, Siobhan O'Conlan, Cathleen O'Connor, and Clare Tregaskis.

Peter Clough and Cathy Nutbrown
Sheffield 2002

Peter Clough and Cathy Nutbrown are Senior Lecturers at
The University of Sheffield, School of Education, UK.
http://www.shef.ac.uk/education

Foreword

In educational research and, more generally, in the social sciences, 'methodology' is taken to be a discipline whose function is to examine the underlying rationale for the methods which produce valid knowledge. In this sense, methodology aims to prescribe what are justifiable methods and procedures that ought to be used in the generation and testing of valid knowledge.

Obviously, since knowledge is thought to be valid only if its production conforms to the methods and procedures prescribed by methodology, the prescriptions of methodology cannot themselves be validated by research. Indeed, it is clear that, since conformity to methodologically justified procedures is a prerequisite to producing valid knowledge, methodology's claim to know what these procedures are presupposes a special kind of knowledge that is in some sense superior to that produced through research. Access to this special kind of knowledge is usually taken to be provided by philosophy. 'Methodology' then presupposes a particular kind of relationship between philosophy and research in which one (philosophy) is able to judge and validate the claims to knowledge advanced by the other (research). Just as research methods are justified by methodology, so research methodologies are justified by philosophy.

Many research theses and dissertations are undertaken by research students with little serious examination of the methodological principles that justify the research methods that have been used. Because of this, the reasons why certain methods were employed or why the research questions were framed in a particular way remain implicit and undisclosed.

One of the purposes of *A Student's Guide to Methodology* is to help students to untangle the connection between methods and methodology, and so help them to make their methodological preconceptions more explicit and more open to critical reflection. It has been written by two researchers who, by drawing on their own research experiences and their extensive experience of teaching research students, outline a process which will enable students to develop a more reflective and critical approach to their research.

As such, Clough and Nutbrown, in this book, meet a real need and make a significant contribution to the argument for research to become a more reflective practice whose practitioners engage in a continuous process of thinking about how they justify their research methods and practices.

Professor Wilfred Carr

Preface: How to Read this Book

What this book is

This book has grown directly out of research teaching sessions we have led with Masters and PhD students over the last ten years, as well as from our own research studies. The idea for it came from our realisation that students were coming up year after year with the same sorts of questions about quite what *methodology* is, and how it differs from *method*. It seemed to us that these questions often reflected a tacit assumption that you carried out your study – using 'methods' – and that you finally wrote something called a 'methodology'. This is an understandable assumption, presumably arising from the traditional requirements of the research dissertation or thesis, where methodology tends to be seen as something contained within a single chapter which largely reports 'What I did' (with a little bit of 'Why I did it'). But accounts like this often do little justice to the constant and endless decision-making processes that are a daily part of any research study worth reporting.

What we developed from these teaching sessions and tutorials is a programme of activities and readings designed to 'turn up the light' on critical decision-making, and many of these now appear in this book. We show how the processes of making methodology are indispensably taking place at all stages of the research – from early, fitful interests or hunches through to the crafting of the final sentence. At all stages decisions are being made, whether it be about the framing of a key research question, the selection of a method, or even the use of a single word. Many of these decisions are of course implicit or otherwise unconscious. The emphasis in the book, then, is on developing a critical approach at all stages, so that it becomes clear in any research report that what the researcher chose to do was not only appropriate, but *necessary*; we see this as the hallmark of persuasive rather than merely adequate methodology.

Our book does not deal with research methods in any detail; there are already many excellent accounts widely available (and we offer guidance to these in Appendix II to the book). Rather, the book is concerned with developing a critical research approach more generally; that is, with the more radical and profound processes of enquiry that lie behind the selection or creation of any given method.

Through a series of activities and readings, the book is effectively a course in *developing critical research sensibility*. From our own teaching and research supervision we know that students who repeatedly confront their own and others' thinking with awkward questions produce more persuasive and effective research studies. More specifically, students who develop to the point of instinct the critical need to justify their enquiry to themselves at every stage have little difficulty with their final account of methodology: it becomes for them a matter of making concrete for others what has been critically at work throughout the study.

To this end, we would urge readers to record responses to some of the activities in a research journal; we should expect that some of this writing would find its way – in some form – into your final dissertation or thesis. We estimate that if you carry out the activities as we suggest throughout this book you will write around 5,000 words which can be used as part of the articulation of the methodology of your study.

The organisation of the text

We have organised this book in three parts. In Part 1 'Research is methodology', we present our working definitions which inform the discussions, examples and activities suggested in the remainder of the book. First we focus on what we see as essential characteristics of social and educational research, then we set out what we mean when we talk about methodology. These two chapters are important because they set the frame of the book as a whole and introduce key themes which permeate Parts II and III. They also contain a number of activities which, if you work through them, will help you to develop your own responses to our definitions and suggestions about the nature of social and educational research and methodological positions and decisions. However you decide to work through the rest of the book, we suggest that you work through Chapters 1 and 2 first.

In Part II 'The pervasive nature of methodology' we open up and exemplify the themes introduced in Part 1 and focus (in Chapters 3–6) on: radical looking, radical listening, radical reading and radical questioning. In this part of the book you may well choose to attend more particularly to one chapter than to others, depending on the structure and thrust of your own study. The order in which you work through these four is not crucial – though there are instances where we refer back to ideas covered in an earlier chapter in so far as they relate to the present discussion. You may prefer to work through these chapters in the sequence in which they are presented, but we have written the chapters in Part II in such a way as to make it possible for you to use them out of sequence if your immediate concerns, as they relate to your particular study, suggest that this would better suit your needs.

The concluding part of the book focuses on the processes involved in producing research for a public audience. In Part III 'Making research public' we focus first on research design, showing (in Chapter 7) how the processes of social enquiry discussed in Part II can influence the shape and scope of any study. In Chapter 8, we invite you to explore the processes and possibilities of writing the research report, using two examples from our own research to demonstrate how social and educational research might be reported so that it remains *persuasive, purposive, positional* and *political*. Finally, in Chapter 9, we suggest how you might use your work in your research journal to plan the next steps in your enquiry.

Keeping a research journal

An important feature of this book is its interactive nature. Our own work with students studying for Higher and Research degrees leads us to believe that it is through responding to text as well as reading those texts that prompts their thinking. So, we suggest that, as you begin to read this book, you also begin a research journal. Every chapter in the book includes activities designed to help you to reflect on the ideas we are discussing. Many activities ask you to respond, in writing, to a particular statement or article and at some points in the book we suggest that you make an observation or reflect on a particular scenario. These can all be recorded in your research journal.

A research journal can take many forms. Some prefer to keep their journal electronically – keeping their thoughts, puzzles, worries, notes, serendipitous discoveries of references, reflections on conversations and points to raise with their supervisor on a single disc. Others use the opening of a new research journal as an excuse to visit the stationery shop to indulge in the purchase of a new notebook – a sort of ritual to mark the start of the enquiry! The style and form of the research journal is a personal matter, because the contents, the structure of those contents, and ultimately the use of those contents will be a personal decision. (No one but you will see your research journal unless you choose to share it with them.) What is important as you begin your research journal is that you choose a format which will make it easy for you to use.

Many of you will be familiar with the idea of keeping a research journal – for some readers this may well be a new idea (or an idea you've heard of but never really adopted). Whenever we suggest the idea of a research journal to our students they always welcome some illustration of what a research journal might look like. So, the example on the next page – taken from one of our own research journals – provides an indication of the kinds of things you might include in your own. This particular journal was begun as a way of thinking through some initial ideas for a research project based on ideas about childhood, children's rights and constructions of childhood and learning difficulty. This represents beginning thoughts, before the formulation of research questions or even a firm notion of the nature or scope of the study. This journal was started in order to work out some of those ideas and, as you will see, includes starting points from various sources. The original journal was handwritten and also contained pasted-in newspaper cuttings, scraps from other notebooks and photographs from magazines.

Thursday 5th February 1998	Article in 'The Leader' *A Special Victory :Parents win dyslexic tribunal case . . .*	Parent 'He would also have had the benefit of a highly qualified and expert teacher and a special lap top computer as well as a work programme approved by the Dyslexia Institute'
		'The cost to the LEA will be £13,000 a year compared to the £5,000 it would have cost to keep him at a mainstream school'
Thursday 12th February 1998	Advertisement in The Leader 'Shape a future for children: can you help Him?'	'John is a seven year old boy who cannot live with his family. He has suffered a lot of moves which have made him feel unsettled and rejected . . .' Nottingham County Council
	Adam Phillips *The Beast in the Nursery* 1998 Faber and Faber	'Children dream but adults want to, indeed need to, teach them; children know what interests them, but adults want them educated' p.59
	Miller, M.L. Manning, P.K. and van Maanen, J. (1993) Editors note in the introduction to Richard G. Mitchell, Jr's book *Secrecy and Fieldwork London: SAGE* Get hold of a copy Theodore Zeldin-An Intimate history of Human Nature? (something like that . . .)	'Like it or not, we are no different from anyone else. We are secretive, and we selectively conceal and reveal' (p.v)
14th March 1998	Conversation with M (age 4:4) Me: You have teachers at school don't you M: Yes, Mrs B . . . and Miss H . . . Me: What do they do? M: Help us, be nice to us . . . Oh! and they give us things to do – things that are interesting – so we learn things	Reflection: First and foremost the teachers are there to nurture – to 'help' to 'be nice' – could we say 'to care' M adds (almost as an afterthought) information about curriculum . . .
April 4th	Proust: Swann's Way *The facts of life do not Penetrate to the sphere In which our beliefs are Cherished: they did not Engender those beliefs, And they are powerless To destroy them*	

Continued overleaf

April 11th	Pedagogy: Establishing rights Understanding needs Realising opportunities	
	St.Pierre, E.A. (1997) Methodology in the fold and the interruption of transgressive data *Qualitative Studies in Education 10, 2, 175–189*	Copy on file. -out-of-category data
May 29th	From Alice's Adventures in Wonderland ... Carroll, L 1865 'Come, let's hear some of your adventures'. 'I could tell you my adventures – beginning from this morning', said Alice a little timidly, ' but it's no use going back to yesterday, because I was a different person then'	This seemed to suggest to me something about research changing researchers – it is as if they are a different person? ...

Example of a research journal

Your research journal is your own creation; as you will see from the example above, there are no rules about what goes in a research journal. It is often useful to date entries – especially if they relate to visits to your research setting and meetings with your academic tutor or supervisor. But the point of a research journal is that it helps you to develop your own ideas about research. The example above is taken from the opening of a journal where ideas and stimuli for a research project from all aspects of experience are recorded as they strike the researcher as relevant (however obliquely). Much of this may well be discarded in the final event of designing and reporting a study, but it is always advisable to hold on to ideas that might seem important, even if at the time you do not know why.

Further reading

Each chapter ends with some suggestions for taking further the ideas and practices discussed. Additionally, we have appended a select Annotated Bibliography which points to useful, often authoritative reading in methods and methodology. We hope that these will be helpful – and that our book will help you respond critically to them!

Peter Clough and Cathy Nutbrown
Sheffield 2002

PART 1

Research is Methodology

What is Research?

CHAPTER CONTENTS

LEARNING OBJECTIVES

By studying and doing the activities in this chapter you will:

◇ be able to define 'research'

◇ respond to the view that social research is persuasive, purposive, positional and political

◇ articulate the purposive nature of research in the social sciences

◇ have reflected on the capacity of research in influence change

◇ be able to express the reasons for doing your own research study

◇ articulate the potential of your own research to 'make a difference'.

Introduction

> All social research sets out with specific *purposes* from a
> particular *position*, and aims to *persuade* readers of the
> significance of its claims; these claims are always broadly *political.*

This definition is our starting point in this book. You may not agree with it, but we hope that by the end of this chapter you will be able to express the extent to which you do, and criticise those aspects that you disagree with.

The chapter is organised around four statements which identify what we see as characteristic of social and educational research. The chapter 'unpacks' these statements, and invites you to make your own responses to them. As we said in the Preface, these responses will contribute directly to the development of your own research methodology.

We think it important to begin this book by encouraging you to set out what *you* mean by research because it is this which underpins your research study and the decisions you will make within it (just as for us, our own definitions of research directly influence our research design and methodological positions). In this book we are addressing issues for those who are developing research studies for higher and research degrees; thus, this first section will focus on what we mean by research in the context of academic study for the purposes of academic awards.

The purpose of much research at Masters or PhD level is not so much to *prove* things – but more to *investigate* questions and *explore* issues. Many researchers either want to understand a situation more clearly or to change things by virtue of their research – some want to do both. But all research, necessarily, is about asking questions, exploring problems and reflecting on what emerges in order to make meaning from the data and tell the research story. As such, research is also a moral act within which the researcher holds responsibility for ensuring that resulting change is 'for the better'; in this sense researchers work for the social 'good'.

Social research is persuasive

> Why would you want to carry out a piece of research if you
> didn't in some way want to *persuade* somebody of the value of
> what you are doing?

How does research 'persuade'? To answer this question, we start here by looking at what counts as research for different people: how, that is, research is defined in relation to its capacity to bring about change.

Activity 1.1

Take some time to think about the following deceptively simple question; it is asked to help you articulate what *you* mean by research.

What is 'research'?

Make a few notes in your research journal in response to this question.

Over the years we have been asking our own students to think about their response to the question in Activity 1.1. They have responded in different ways. The following list gives some students' written responses to the same question:

- Research is the investigation of an idea, subject or topic for a purpose. It enables the researcher to extend knowledge or explore theory. It offers the opportunity to investigate an area of interest from a particular perspective.
- The methods you use to obtain information from a variety of sources.
- Investigation and discovery. An opportunity to investigate a theory that requires further interpretation and greater understanding.
- A rigorous enquiry about an area which is of interest for various reasons, e.g. it may be an area about which little is known, or an area which is causing concern.
- Discovery, finding out, study, looking in depth, investigation, reaching new ideas/conclusions.
- The term research is for me a way of describing a systematic investigation of a phenomenon or area of activity. It can sometimes be accurately measured scientifically or data collected can be analysed and compared to identify trends, similarities or differences.

Activity 1.2

We have listed below the terms used in the above definitions of research. Glance through the list and then look back to the definition you wrote in your response to Activity 1.1. Are any of the terms listed here included in your own definition? Are any of them useful to you in revising your definition? Make some notes – in your research journal – on any changes you've made and what you've learned about your own thinking about research.

concern	conclusions
depth	discovery

---

enquiry	explore theory
extend knowledge	finding out
idea	information
interpretation	investigation
measure	new ideas
opportunity	perspective
purpose	rigorous
subject	systematic
topic	trends
understanding	

Thus we have seen, through the words of our students, how crucial it is when doing research to maintain an idea of making a difference in some way to something. In the next section we shall look at the purposive nature of social research.

Social research is purposive

> There is little point in carrying out a research project
> (whatever the scale) if there is no ultimate aim to achieve
> something as a result.

As you have seen, our students' descriptions of research convey a strong sense of finding out, of *purposive* enquiry. The task of researchers to 'find out' is stressed by Goodwin and Goodwin (1996) who emphasise the generation of knowledge, solving of problems and better understanding:

> In a general sense, research means finding out . . . the types, or methods have in common the generation of knowledge at varying levels of detail, sophistication, and generalizability. Research results in the creation of knowledge to solve a problem, answer a question, and better describe or understand something. In all these instances, producing new knowledge highlights the research process aimed at finding out. (Goodwin and Goodwin, 1996: 5)

This is not surprising, because, as the following discussion demonstrates, what is important to those who carry out research – whatever its scale – is that it should somehow *make a difference*.

In the following group tutorial various definitions of 'research' are offered and discussed. Focus, as you read, on the ideas which emerge about:

- the *meaning of the term* 'research'
- what research should *accomplish*.

Group tutorial: What do we mean by 'research'?

In preparation for this tutorial the students were asked to write down their response to the question 'What is research?'. They draw on their written notes in the discussion which follows.

SN   Okay, well . . . what I've written here is/it probably sounds, really/I don't know . . . Okay, 'Research is a process of purposeful, in-depth investigation of a particular issue. It follows a defined structured approach to obtain answers which make useful contributions to knowledge or to practice'.

Tutor   So, research is a process – has to be purposeful, and make a contribution to knowledge, OK. But this definition goes on to make us ask a number of questions, such as: what do you mean by 'in-depth', does research have to follow a 'defined structured approach'? Does it always have to find 'answers'?

AM   Well I've got a note here about . . . well . . . I understand the term to mean looking into an issue that is of interest, or needs analysis, in great detail. By doing this, the issue becomes clearer, is easier to explain and, if it's contentious, becomes more easily resolved. Researching an area helps to tease out the problems and make the picture clearer. This should help focus on the areas that need more work. I was thinking about my problem with focusing in on precise questions there, I think . . .

MT   Mmm . . . It's difficult isn't it? When you have to pin it down. I've got a note about, well, I said 'To take a particular issue that is specific and possibly innovative to study in depth' – that's what I think research is . . . and I said that 'Results can be interpreted by the perspective of others – it stimulates debate and further issues for consideration'.

Tutor   So, research leads to clarification of issues – and ideas? – and leads to the generation of yet more issues to be considered? Could we say that research often generates more questions than answers?

CT   Possibly, but it does provide a means of finding out about issues of concern or areas of interest. When I was thinking about this I said that it was 'Drawing together a variety of thoughts and opinions in order to move these issues or interests forward and therefore build upon the research findings'. I think research is about encouraging other professionals to challenge or just become interested enough to find out more – so yes – more questions but also some 'responses' to issues . . . some answers.

MM   It is about generating understanding, greater awareness of an idea, achieving additional knowledge and meaning – isn't it?

Tutor   So, what's emerging here is the importance of research as an *organising structure*, a means by which a body of knowledge is assembled in response to questions and new knowledge generated.

SN   Yes, research is often an investigation which is used to gather information. In my notes I wrote . . . 'To gain new knowledge and to confirm, or disprove information already known'.

Tutor   So one of the purposes of research is to check out existing assumptions? What about the role of research in bringing about change?

MM   Yes, for example a lot of research is usually an investigation into a topic which is then evaluated. And there are links between educational research and policy-making – those kinds of studies sometimes lead to change in a Local Authority for example. My key thing about research was that . . . 'Research informs events and allows for critical appraisal of the findings'. That's what I wrote.

CT   Research needs to affect thinking and/or practice.

SN   Research can also reveal the unexpected!

Activity 1.3

Before you move on – take some time to think about the following question. It is designed to help you articulate *your* reasons for doing the particular research study *you* have chosen.

What is the purpose of *your* research study?

We asked 114 of our students attending a study school to write down their reasons for undertaking the study they had chosen. The 97 students who responded gave us answers which we sorted into the following six categories:

- to bring about change
- because it was commissioned by funders
- for interest
- to get a qualification
- for self-development
- for understanding.

Of the 97 students 82 gave a single reason for undertaking their research and the remaining 15 gave two reasons. The reasons given by the students are ranked in order of importance in Table 1.1.

We do not take the outcomes of this small survey to mean that few of our students are interested in gaining their higher degree or that only 17 of the 97 were interested in their work! We could say that getting the degree is a 'taken-for-granted' reason! What *is* interesting is that important factors for these students were the opportunity to bring about *change* – to make a difference; their own self-development as professionals and the chance to develop new or deeper understandings.

Table 1.1   *Responses of students to the question 'Why are you doing this piece of research?'*

Category	Number of responses (n=97)
Change	30
Self-development	29
Understanding	27
Interest	17
Commissioned	5
Qualification	5

These are examples of their comments:

Researching to bring about change

To find out how I can make a difference to practice in order that children's well-being, their learning and their group identity will be improved.

To enhance my work with children 'at risk'.

Researching for self-development

To challenge some of my own ideas.

To extend my own thinking.

To improve the way I do my job.

To increase my professional development and understanding.

Researching for understanding

To develop a greater understanding of pupils' learning in collaboration with their parents.

To gather background information on how gender is affected by different social and economic backgrounds through a solid review of what's been done already, and then to gather together new information obtained through questionnaires and informal interviews.

To gain a more in-depth understanding of the people in my team whom I support. I want to understand more of their backgrounds, attitudes towards students, education and their relationships with other workers in the field.

So, students often carry out research with the expressed purpose of bringing about some kind of change – in the situation they are researching, in themselves and in their own understanding.

Activity 1.4

Look back at your own response to the question in Activity 1.3.
Are your reasons for carrying out your own study reflected in the categories we identified in Table 1.1? Do you have a different reason? This is an important point of reflection, because if you are clear about your research rationale you will be better able to highlight your own particular motivational factors and articulate those in your written report.

Social research is positional

Research which did not express a more or less distinct perspective on the world would not be research at all; it would have the status of a telephone directory where data are listed without analysis.

Research *becomes* research when its written report is made public (Stenhouse, 1975) thus giving expression to the standpoint of its authors in a given context. It is the context in which research is (first) conducted and (finally) reported which gives it its real meaning. Research – at least educational and social science research – does not take place in isolation. People drive research, they identify the emerging issues to be studied and they create – in context – the methods by which situations are further understood, and they communicate its outcomes to chosen audiences. As Hannon has it, research takes place in the contexts of its community environment, in interaction with the rest of life. He suggests that we: 'Think of educational research as a living plant in interaction with its environment – constantly review-ing itself, sometimes growing, sometimes declining . . .' (Hannon, 1998: 150). This ecological perspective on research encourages the idea of research *itself* changing as wider social contexts and needs for understanding change. The ways in which we choose to conduct our enquiry, the nature of our questions and the moral intents are expressions of our positionality and will govern the ways in which we craft and change the research act itself.

Several examples of the development of research, particularly in relation to its geographical and political local contexts, can be found in Clough and Nutbrown

(2001), which reports the methodology and findings of a number of small-scale studies completed by Masters' students. Each of the reports emphasises the importance of the context within which the study took place, and those contexts shaped the research questions, the methodological frames and the nature of the reports. For example, Koch's study (Koch, 2001) on the factors which influence young women students' choices of post-secondary education was constructed in the context of its location in the Arabian Gulf. Within that context the research needed to understand and take account of (and ultimately gain expression in) the balance of local and expatriate population and of the political, religious, cultural and economic realities of life in the Gulf States. Similarly a report by Parackal (2001) examines the perspectives of teachers of children with special educational needs in Beirut, Lebanon. This study is particularly informed and shaped by its context, and must be interpreted in the context of the social structure of the country with the civil war of 1974–89 seriously affecting educational developments in the country. Thus the need to research particular issues grows from the contexts in which the researcher operates, and what is an appropriate research question in one context often lacks relevance in others. For example, Khan (2002) studied the development of strategies for managing the behaviour of young children in kindergartens in Trinidad and Tobago without recourse to corporal punishment. This study took place in the context of a developing country where the death penalty was still in operation and where the beating and physical chastisement of children at home and in schools was not out of the ordinary – but where issues of children's rights were beginning to form part of the educational/social agenda. Khan's rationale for her study was born out of a professional and political context and was 'of the moment' in that context. Her clear moral and political position provided both her motivation for carrying out the study and the organising structure of her final report.

Activity. 1.5   Your research contexts

We have given some examples of studies which have arisen out of the specific moral and physical contexts in which students have found themselves.
Your research report will need to include some picture of these contexts as they relate to your own study. Write 2–300 words now, which begin to map out these factors.
Consider:

What is the political context?
What is the social context in which it will take place?
Are there religious and/or political factors which will influence your research questions or your research design?
How might these factors shape your research study?

Social research is political

> Research which changes nothing – not even the researcher – is not research at all. And since all social research takes place in policy contexts of one form or another research itself must therefore be seen as inevitably political.

There was a strong sense in the tutorial discussion (on page 7) that it is what research *achieves* that gives it its definition. If we were to say 'research *is* x', it would carry very little meaning; in fact, Blaxter, Hughes and Tight (2001:4) present a somewhat simplistic (and we suspect 'tongue-in-cheek') list in response to the question 'Research is . . .' They ask readers to think about statements such as, 'Research . . . is about: proving your pet theory . . . is done by academics . . . is about establishing facts . . . is objective . . . is about justifying what your funder wants to do . . . can prove anything you want . . . is time-consuming . . . is scientific . . . is removed from reality . . . cannot change anything'.

Such statements do not reach to the heart of the issue, but rather take us nowhere; in fact, they divert us from the identification of the central argument about the capacity of educational and social research to influence change. But to say 'this research has changed this . . .' or 'that study made a difference to . . .' is the important defining feature. So, research worthy of the name must bring about some change: change in the researcher, change in the researched, change in the user of research.

Activity 1.6

Think of a research paper which you have read recently.

What was it that the research study changed?
What impact did it have?
On whom?
On what?

Having ascertained that most of our students want their research to bring about some (however modest) kind of change, we asked them to tell us briefly what difference they thought their research could make. All 97 students responded that something would happen as a result of their research. Their responses fell into four broad categories of change:

- policy
- practice
- professional development
- stimulus for further research.

Students' expectations for the impact of their research studies are ranked, in order of expressed importance, in Table 1.2.

Table 1.2   *Students' expectations of the impact of their research on policy, practice or professional development ranked in order of expressed importance*

Students' expectation that their research would make a difference in the area of . . .	Number of responses (n=97)
Practice (personal/professional)	51
Professional development	32
Policy (institution/local/national)	11
Stimulus for further research	3

There is a sense here of a desire for *action*, of students wanting to put the outcomes of their research to some practical operation They said:

Of making a difference to policy

Studies on the impact of Ofsted inspection on practice are few, therefore, my research will contribute to knowledge on this area.

Education Services can be very focused on 'educating the child'. I would like to highlight the issues around perspective, contribution and values of parents as a policy factor.

May be useful in policy development and the procurement of resources.

Of making a difference to practice

My research will reflect my own practice, and in the way I train others.

I hope the research will inform future practice in work with people with learning difficulties.

I hope it will increase continuity of activities between multidisciplinary agencies working with women in the community.

I'm planning to use it to develop new guidelines for the induction of new staff into the Unit.

Of making a difference to professional development

. . . it will give me a better understanding of what I do.

It should influence the attitudes and perceptions of colleagues.

The greatest difference I can hope it will make will be in terms of personal differences to my understanding and attitudes.

I hope it will influence/provoke thought in other professionals about issues of gender and exclusion.

Policy, practice and professional development are all politically oriented or motivated arenas and the students' desire to influence developments in these areas of work is – in itself – political.

Activity 1.7   What difference could your research make?

Having reflected on the areas of change which our students have highlighted, think about your own research and what you want to achieve. Now, in your research journal, respond to the same question:

What difference could your research make?

Remember that what you want to achieve will directly determine your methodology. Your considered response to this question will underpin many of the research decisions you take.

Traditions of enquiry: false dichotomies

Looking back over your notes and writings made during your reading of this chapter, how do you now respond to our opening statement that:

> All social research sets out with specific *purposes* from a particular *position*, and aims to *persuade* readers of the significance of its claims; these claims are always broadly *political*.

It has been argued (Carr, 1995) that distinct paradigms and scientific method are less appropriate for educational research for this creates a demand for divisions between researchers and teachers. Naturalism (or normative) and interpretive approaches, he argues, should be repudiated and the development of research that is 'both educational and scientific' should be the goal.

Just as it may erroneously seem that research methods are simply and readily 'to hand', research is similarly often characterised uncritically in terms of polarisations: it is qualitative or quantitative, or else it is *positivist* or *interpretative* and so on. The emergence of *critical theory* in educational research offers a third paradigm, linked with the political stance of emancipation of individuals and groups within society.

Critical theorists would thus argue that their work is *transformative* in that it seeks to change people and societies. But in terms of the research process – of what actually happens when people *make* research – these paradigms are ultimately no more than *post hoc* descriptions of gross characterisation. In addressing a task we do not immediately go to adopt this or that methodology as such; rather, we again confront specific problems which we come eventually to locate in continually related – rather than opposed – ways of construing the world.

Denscombe (1998: 3) states that 'the social researcher is faced with a variety of options and alternatives and has to make strategic decisions about which to choose'. He suggests six key issues should be taken into account when making decisions about the viability of social science research: relevance; feasibility; coverage; accuracy; objectivity and ethics. A series of questions are posed (under each of these six headings) for researchers to ask at the planning stage of their project. We suggest a seventh factor should be included in this checklist, that of *interest and motivation*, because research projects become part of the life of researchers and it is important that any research 'grabs' the researcher sufficiently to sustain them throughout the study and all its triumphs and disasters!

Some writers continue to support the separation of research paradigm. Cohen, Manion and Morrison (2000) offer the following scheme of what they see as contrasting approaches to research; specifically, normative, interpretive and critical paradigm.

The scheme in Table 1.3 serves to provide broad, *post hoc* frameworks for characterising the means and concerns of any given study; but it must be clear that in practice – in making research as part of a lived world – it is not possible to study 'society and the social system' without at least some interactive notion of and reference to 'the individual'; or to 'generalise from the specific' without in some way 'interpreting [that] specific'.

Hence the idea of choice *between* broad approaches characterised in this way is ultimately spurious and as Merton and Kendall (1986: 549) point out, the real choice is that combination of both which makes use of the most valuable features of each. The problem becomes one of determining *at which points* they should 'adopt the one and at which the other approach.'

Activity 1.8

Study Table 1.3 in which Cohen, Manion and Morrison summarise three paradigms for research. Thinking about your own study, consider where you would locate your work in relation to those paradigms. Would you say your work lies within a normative, interpretive or critical paradigm? Does it help to describe your work in such terms? How does such a location help you to make methodological decisions? Write a paragraph or so in your research journal in response to these questions.

Table 1.3   *Differing approaches to the study of behaviour*

Normative	Interpretative	Critical
Society and the social system	The individual	Societies, groups, individuals
Medium/large-scale research	Small-scale research	Small-scale research
Impersonal, anonymous forces regulating behaviour	Human actions continuously re-creating social life	Political, ideological factors, power and interest shaping behaviours
Model of natural sciences	Non-statistical	Ideology critique and action research
'Objectivity'	'Subjectivity'	'Collectivity'
Research conducted 'from the outside'	Personal involvement of the researcher	Participant researchers, researchers and facilitators
Generalising from the specific	Interpreting the specific	Critiquing the specific
Explaining the behaviour/ seeking causes	Understanding actions/ meanings rather than causes	Understanding, interrogating, critiquing, transforming actions and interests
Assuming the taken-for-granted	Investigating the taken-for-granted	Interrogating and critiquing the taken-for-granted
Macro-concepts: society, institutions, norms, positions, roles, expectations	Micro-concepts: individual perspective, constructs, negotiated, meanings, definitions of situations	Macro- and micro-concepts: political and ideological interests, operations of power
Structuralists	Phenomenologists, symbolic interactionists, ethnomethodologists,	Critical theorists, action researchers, practitioner researchers
Technical interest	Practical interest	Emancipatory interest

Source: Cohen, Manion and Morrison, 2000: 35

We can dig deeper into this realm of separate research paradigm and uncover further argument about the relationship between research design and various research methods. With the wide range of texts on research methods currently available (see Appendix II) there is a wealth of opinion on record. Let us consider one further position at this point. Writing about research design in social research, de Vaus argues:

Failing to distinguish between design and method leads to poor evaluation of designs. Equating cross-sectional designs with questionnaires, or case studies with participant observation, means that the designs are often evaluated against the strengths and weaknesses of the method rather than their ability to draw relatively unambiguous conclusions or to select between rival plausible hypotheses.

Similarly, designs are often equated with qualitative and quantitative research methods. Social surveys and experiments are frequently viewed as prime examples of quantitative research and are evaluated against the strengths and weaknesses of statistical, quantitative research methods and analysis. Case studies, on the other hand, are often seen as prime examples of qualitative research – which adopts an interpretive approach to data, studies 'things' within their context and considers the subjective meanings that people bring to their situation.

It is erroneous to equate a particular research design with either quantitative or qualitative methods. (2001: 9–10)

Activity 1.9

In the light of de Vaus's perspective, review what you wrote in response to Activity 1.8 when you reflected on the Table 1.3 on page 16. Does your writing still reflect your position? Make any changes you think appropriate.

Making method/ology

Decisions about the location of a particular piece of research (or a researcher) within a research paradigm and the selection of methods for research studies can only be made in the light of specific situations and particular phenomena. To be sure, there already exist traditions and 'blueprints' of practice which suggest – more or (often) less critically – ways of proceeding and which frequently condition our view of how phenomena should be investigated. But these should never be seen as techniques which can be lifted wholesale from other accounts and imported uncritically into an enquiry motivated by specifically different situations and subjects.

For research is by definition a *search* for *form* quite as much and at the same time as it has any *content* to report; methods should be seen as being *constructed* (for particular purposes) rather than *selected* (for any general usefulness).

Such a view amplifies the earlier claim that the task of a methodology is to explain the particularity of the methods made for a given study. A characteristic purpose of a methodology is to show not how such and such appeared to be the best method available for the given purposes of the study, but how and why *this way of doing it was unavoidable – was required by – the context and purpose of this particular enquiry.*

Thus, we suggest that methodological considerations stem from the obvious; that different researchers can offer different interpretations of the same data. Methodology requires researchers to *justify* their *particular* research decisions, from the outset to the conclusion of their enquiry.

The final difference between a persuasive and a merely sufficient methodology is that the convincing one takes little for granted. It worries endlessly at its own terms and is not content to justify its decisions largely by reference to other research. To be sure, research must be contextualised in terms of what other enquirers have claimed as findings (and it is normally the job of a literature review to do most of this) but it should also be located – and justified – in terms of an argument about the very nature and structure of knowledge and knowing.

Activity 1.10

Consider the following statement:

'Method' in social science subverts a profound human impulse to tell stories about the world as we see it. Method undoes the truth, for we put in method a trust it could not start to understand, being without feeling. We ask method to do something – to validate our work – which we cannot do ourselves. All method can do – or at least method as we know it in the social sciences – all method can do is reflect back to us our lack of engagement with our work, a lack we must announce as the very condition of our professionalism. (Clough, 1995: 126)

Consider these questions:

- Is research opposed to lived experience in this way?
- Does research *have* to be methodical?
- Can there be such a thing as research which is *not* methodical?
- Do certain methods carry with them certain values?
- To what extent are the values of the researcher inevitably present in her work?

Drawing on your answers to these questions, write an account, in not more than 1,000 words, in response to the above statement.

Remember that the pieces you write in response to the activities in this chapter may well be incorporated into your dissertation or thesis.

Many popular texts on research methods offer information on 'contrasting' approaches (for example Cohen, Manion and Morrison). Indeed Denzin and Lincoln continue to denote the 'either/or' response to research paradigm:

> The word qualitative implies an emphasis on the qualities of entities and on processes and meanings that are not experimentally examined or measured (if measured at all) in terms of quantity, amount, intensity, or frequency. Qualitative researchers stress the socially constructed nature of reality, the intimate relationship between the researcher and what is studied, and the situational constraints that shape inquiry. Such researchers emphasise the value-laden nature of inquiry. They seek answers to questions that stress how social experience is created and given meaning. In contrast, quantitative studies emphasise the measurement and analysis of causal relationships between variables, not processes. Proponents of such studies claim that their work is done from within a value-free framework. (2000: 8)

But in reality, many researchers in education and the social sciences do not select one research paradigm to investigate all their questions, choosing *either* a normative *or* interpretive approach. In our own work we have – during the course of our research careers – worked within both positivist and interpretivist paradigms. Would we want to describe ourselves as 'either' qualitative 'or' quantitative researchers? The important point here is that we adopt research stances *as they are appropriate to our work*. There are important questions to unpack in the extract above, and perhaps the issue of greatest concern is that of values. Are studies which employ quantitative approaches *necessarily* value-free? Is such a state possible, or desirable? And is it realistic to approach research design by making the choice between 'either' the 'objectivity' of a normative model 'or' the 'subjectivity' of the interpretive model? Research studies often move between these broad approaches selecting the most appropriate for each part of the study. The issue is not so much a question of which paradigm to work within (see Merton and Kendall, 1986) but how to dissolve that distinction in the interests of developing research design which serves the investigation of the questions posed through that research.

If you have worked through the activities in this chapter, making notes and composing paragraphs as we have suggested, you will have written around 2,000 words which can be later incorporated in your dissertation or thesis.

CHAPTER SUMMARY

In this chapter we have:

Encouraged you to reflect on a range of definitions and to develop your own definition of research

Provided an overview of research as persuasive, purposive, positional and political activity

Considered the purposive nature of research

Considered the positional nature of research

Discussed the function of research as a process of political change

Discussed the relationship between research paradigms and the nature of social research as persuasive, purposive, positional and political

📖 FURTHER READING

Clough, P. (1995) 'Problems of identity and method in the investigation of special educational needs', in P. Clough and L. Barton (eds) *Making Difficulties: Research and the Construction of Special Educational Needs*. London: Paul Chapman.

> The organising concept of this chapter is that of identity: the identity of a researcher and the identity of others whose lives occupy the ground of the research. It further supports the work in Activity 1.3.

Clough, P. and Nutbrown, C. (eds) (2001) *Voices of Arabia: Essays in Educational Research*. Sheffield: University of Sheffield Papers in Education.

> This collection contains reports from nine Masters students drawn on their Masters' dissertations. It illustrates issues discussed in the 'Social research is positional' section on research contexts.

What is Methodology?

CHAPTER CONTENTS

LEARNING OBJECTIVES

By studying the contents of this chapter and doing the activities you will:

◇ be able to articulate what is meant by the term 'methodology'

◇ eliminate confusion between 'methods' and 'methodology'

◇ understand why methodological issues are important considerations for your own research study

◇ understand the central role of 'research questions'

◇ be able to compose and justify your own research questions

◇ Write some 300 or so words which you can later use to discuss your research questions and the methodological justification for the mode of enquiry you have chosen to investigate them.

What do we mean by 'methodology'?

> A methodology shows how research questions are articulated with questions asked in the field. Its effect is a claim about significance . . .

This chapter addresses an issue which many people coming new to research find confusing, and that is the difference between methods and methodology. We suggest that, at its simplest, this distinction can be seen in terms of *methods* as being some of the ingredients of research, whilst *methodology* provides the *reasons* for using a particular research recipe.

The chapter explores the relationship of methods and methodology, and the ongoing task of *justification* which a methodology represents. Thus methodology starts quite simply by asking questions such as: '*Why* interview?', '*Why* carry out a questionnaire survey?', '*Why* interview 25 rather than 500 participants?'. Decisions such as these are apparently often practical, but they carry very deep, often unarticulated, implications. They are often based on values and assumptions which influence the study, and as such therefore need to be fully interrogated in order to clarify the research decisions which are made. The implications of research decisions are often not fully realised (or perhaps realised too late, when data have already been collected). They are often unexplained, and in many cases poorly justified.

Activity 2.1   What is methodology?

Write a short definition of what you understand by *methodology*. We will return to your definition later in the chapter.

'The arrest of experience'

Research puts common experience into brackets, makes 'objects' of experience so that they can be examined and understood. One of the things which research requires people to do is to question assumptions and perceptions which are taken for granted in the normal run of everyday life; Michael Oakeshott (1933) described this as an 'arrest of experience', when we try to step outside our everyday experience of people, objects and places, and subject them to different sorts of examination. Oakeshott reminds us that 'Nature is the *product* not the evidence of scientific thought' (1933: 191). The information becomes, then, not the *consequence* of a way of seeing even, but that *act* itself (an 'object'), and as such must be intentionally opposed to the thing in itself. In this opposition we discover the *nature of the particular*. For science attempts to conceive of the world in defined categories and its datum has the required stability only by virtue of the categorical set of which it is an indifferent member. There can, by this definition, be no such scientific experience as that *of the particular*.

Whatever actual methods are ultimately employed in a study, we suggest that the 'arrest of experience' – present in all research studies – can be characterised by four forms of *radical enquiry*. These are *radical looking, radical listening, radical reading* and *radical questioning*.

Radical looking:

> *Radical looking* is the means by which research process makes the familiar strange, and gaps in knowledge are revealed

---

What we mean by *radical looking* is exploration beyond the familiar and the (personally) known, to the roots of a situation: this is *exploration which makes the familiar strange*.

All researchers need to develop the capacity to see their topic with new and different lenses, in order to look beyond and transform their own current knowledge. Topics present themselves for research in different ways, and for all sorts of different reasons. What distinguishes research from everyday interest or curiosity, however, is the opening up of familiar things to alternative ways of seeing. Thus an *interest* in, say, adolescent drug culture only starts to become *research* proper when that curiosity is *systematically informed by perspectives outside of the researcher's normal vision*: what is already known about this topic? What have other researchers found? Are there policy contexts which affect this culture? What do adolescents themselves think about the situation? And, most importantly, what are the gaps and can I add to the public state of knowledge?

Answers to these – and many other such – questions do not simply describe the situation under enquiry, filling in informational blanks, as it were. They actually refine and define the topic: this sort of radical looking at others' knowledge allows researchers to examine and then start to discard information as they begin to focus on a particular problem, a particular *gap in knowledge*. Thus, to stay with the example above, there may be a great deal of relevant work on adolescent drug culture, and it is necessary to be critically aware of this. However, by definition nobody will have carried out your particular study with *these* kids *this* year and in *this* town.

In Chapter 3 we present an example of a research study which illustrates what we mean by 'looking' and interpret the theme both in terms of *radical looking* and some methods of *observation* and their interpretation.

Radical listening:

> *Radical listening* – as opposed to merely hearing – is the interpretative and critical means through which 'voice' is noticed.

What we mean by *radical listening* is a careful attention to all the *voices* which may be heard within and around any given topic. These include both the (literal) voices of research subjects – in interview, for example – and also the voices which are at work in other research reports. This is really part of the same process as radical looking, but it adds emphasis to our view (outlined in Chapter 1) of social research as characteristically *positional* and *political*.

Radical listening, then, involves working out *positionality*. This means trying to understand something of what lies behind what is said by research subjects and written by other researchers; trying to understand this in terms of the speaker's/author's intentions; and trying to understand what this means within their particular social frameworks. If you accept our argument in Chapter 1 that all research is political, then it follows that whatever evidence you take from research subjects, or other research writers, embodies a particular political position (however implicit this may be). This is what we mean here by 'voice'.

Activity 2.2

Make some notes about:

- what counts as 'voice'?
- why do you want to listen?
- what do you want to hear?
- do you want to listen to what you hear?

The articulation of responses to the above questions will provide you with your rationale for the *methods* of listening which you choose to use in your own studies.

The methodological issues raised by the decision to collect and analyse data which elicit many voices of participants are important. Whether carrying out ethnographic studies or large surveys which involve listening to others' voices in research studies, the justification for listening to a range of voices in a variety of dimensions must be made clear. We shall see more of this in Chapter 4, which includes an example of a study designed to elicit a number of voices. In this example the methodological 'frame' is as interesting as the substantive 'findings' (or outcomes) of the research. Radical listening, we suggest, should be central to any form of research whatever its substantive content or paradigm.

Radical reading:

> *Radical reading* provides the justification for the critical adoption
> or rejection of existing knowledge and practices.

In Chapter 1 we showed how social research is *purposive* and *positional*, and we see *radical reading* as a process which exposes the purposes and positions of texts and practices. In this way we are using 'reading' both in a traditional sense – as addressing written texts – and in the metaphorical sense – 'How do *you* read this or that situation?' This process is inseparable from *radical looking* and *radical listening*, but what distinguishes *radical reading* is the notion of *criticality*.

> *Criticality* – 'being critical' – describes the attempt to show *on
> what terms* 'personal' and 'public' knowledges are jointly
> articulated – and therefore where their *positional* differences lie.

A critical account of anything seeks to be *rational*, but cannot fail to reflect the values and beliefs of its author; the most *persuasive* critical accounts reveal the full range of values at work in the analysis.

We shall return to this theme in Chapter 5 with a discussion of the centrality to the research process of the literature search and review and of the less formal 'readings' of the research settings which researchers inevitably make.

Radical questioning:

> *Radical questioning* reveals not only gaps in knowledge but also
> why and how particular answers might be morally and
> politically necessitated.

Radical questioning lies at the heart of a thesis, and brings together the earlier notions of *radically attending* to a topic or situation or events.

All researchers ask questions. They ask sometimes 'innocent' and 'naive' questions about their research focus, as well as searching questions about their data, their processes on analysis, their ethical positions and their moral intent. Research methodology involves, as a minimum, three kinds of questioning activity: personal questions, research questions and field questions.

Personal questions. Researchers must ask questions of themselves about what drives their research and the location of themselves in their research.
Research questions. The careful formulation of 'research questions' – which form the major planks of any research study – is key to the realisation of a successful research study, however large or small.
Field questions. These are quite literally questions which are asked 'in the field'. The formulation of these empirical questions follows the development of research questions and planned acts of data collection in the field should always be directly related to the research questions.

Of course, some research studies will also involve the questioning of research participants, in which case there are further decisions to be made, in terms of: who to ask; what to ask; when to ask; going back again (re-asking); being specific; being open. These form the fine detail of field questions.

In the acts of looking, listening, reading and asking it is also important for researchers to 'get the feel' of their research settings and situations. They need to be sensitive to 'hunches' which they might later investigate, or which might alert them to the need for particular responses to situations. In suggesting that researchers 'feel' their settings we are arguing the need for a holistic response to research design. Chapter 6 further develops these themes.

Activity 2.3

Consider the functions of looking, listening, reading, and questioning in relation to your own (proposed) research study. Which of these tasks might presently seem to have more prominence in your own research?

Do you think that the idea of 'feeling' your research setting has any valid function in the context of your particular study? Make a few notes in your research journal before you move on. You may wish to add to your notes on these topics as you work through the book.

Distinguishing between 'methods' and 'methodology'

> The job of *method* is only to 'hold apart' the researcher and her
> objects, so that we can tell the difference between them.
> Methods do not tell us what the thing is; they do not even
> describe it. All they tell us is the circumstances under which the
> researcher met the object; and they normally seek to provide a
> guarantee that researcher and object are distinct from each
> other. 'Postmodern' accounts say it is impossible to do this.

First we shall discuss the relationship between research methods and methodology, and argue that one of the tasks for a methodology is to explain and justify the particular methods used in a given study.

> Selection of methods may be an act of faith rather than a rational response to a clearly formulated problem. The method may even be an intrinsic part of the problem, rather than extrinsic and disconnected from it. Just as recipes are not simply things that are done to food, but become concepts within which method and substance are compounded, so 'method' in research can become an intrinsic part of the project. The methods we choose are, in this sense, there to be tested, just as much as the substantive hypothesis. (Walker, 1985: 87)

In a sense – a common sense – there is not a deal to say about research methods as such; they are in the end tools, no more, and we may appear to take them from the shelf when we need them.

But methods only – and this is crucial – *only* arise in the service of quite particular needs and purposes. Their usefulness falls away if and as these needs are met and these purposes fulfilled. To be sure, as critical readers of a research report we may wish to know how such and such an insight was arrived at, and hence we may check the researcher's claims to validity and reliability, say, by asking questions of her method. But if the work ultimately has significance for us, it is because its quite particular purpose has been achieved; and to do this, it will have called on the construction of quite particular tools.

It is for this reason that the idea of method as an indifferent tool is seldom borne out by the experience of researchers. A method turns out not to be a spanner – or even a micrometer – but rather something which has to be painstakingly custom-built from other drafters' cast-offs which, whilst providing a general guidance, were not made *for this particular job*. It is actually this particularity which it becomes the task of methodology to explain.

'Choosing' methods?

It is true – if a truism – that channels of communication determine what may pass along them. Research methods observe this rule. A statistical survey, for example, generates one particular form of information at the expense of others, and you would not normally expect to learn much about the *experience* of respondents from this sort of enquiry. Alternatively, an ethnographic study may tell you a great deal about the culture of any given situation and the people involved in it, but you would not easily be able to infer *generalities* about *other* situations from this sort of data.

However, in delimiting the sorts of information which may be accessed, channels of communication – in this case, particular research methods – represent (though often tacitly) differing views on how the world is constructed and how it operates.

Let us take an example of the genesis and development of a piece of research; let us say, for argument's sake, that we wish to find out about the political consciousness of 16–18-year-old students in a tertiary college. Now there is clearly a number of ways in which we could do this, though it would be hard to avoid using one or more from a choice of interview, questionnaire and observation techniques. But the point is that the choice of method will itself depend on much earlier, often tacit, decision-making processes about the *nature* of *knowledge itself*. Are we to assume, for example, that the political beliefs held by our subjects are something which are more or less ready to hand, and which require merely the right question – the appropriate cue – to bring them to expression, and to record? Alternatively, might we assume that a political belief is something which may well be latent, requiring extended and almost certainly interactive interviewing to bring it to light not only to the researcher, but to the subjects themselves? And, in any event, can there be such a thing as context-free and enduring political beliefs, or are they rather tied to specific events?

Or take a different set of questions: however should we select whoever it is we want to interview or issue with a questionnaire or whatever? Why him and not her? Why 25 rather than 105? Or – from later moments in the process of carrying out the research – what will 'count' as evidence, and what be 'discounted'?

And what about our part in the design and carrying out of this study? Can we be 'neutral', be 'objective'? And should we?

Partial answers to all these and the many more questions will be found as functions of our choice of methods; but the coherence and – above all – power to persuade others of our research will derive ultimately from the *painstaking justification we offer for the decisions we have made*.

Activity 2.4

You want to find out the views of employers on employing young people with a criminal record. How will you approach the task?

Will you interview? How many? Who? Where?

Will you carry out a questionnaire survey by post? How many? Who? Where?

Make some notes on your planned strategy and, importantly, *why* you make particular research decisions.

So, we suggest that it is not so much a case of 'choosing' methods as 'making' specifically crafted tools for a specifically generated set of questions which respond to a particular 'problem'. This theme will be addressed through various examples in the book.

What is methodology for?

> A methodology shows how research questions are articulated with questions asked in the field. Its effect is a claim about significance.

Trying to produce a definitive definition of methodology as used in the social sciences, and to serve the purposes of all researchers is rather like trying to catch water in a net. Different researchers offer slightly differing definitions according to their own training, discipline and purposes. Thus Kaplan sees the aim of methodology to be:

> to describe and analyse . . . methods, throwing light on their limitations and resources, clarifying their suppositions and consequences, relating their potentialities to the twilight zone at the frontiers of knowledge. It is to venture generalisations from the success of particular techniques, suggesting new applications, and to unfold the specific bearings of logical and metaphysical principles on concrete problems, suggesting new formulations. (1973: 93)

Miles and Huberman on the other hand, emphasise 'puzzlement' in pointing to the role of methodology:

> In our survey of qualitative researchers, we asked about issues that were unclear and puzzling. One researcher replied: 'Everything is unclear and puzzling . . . Improved methodology, however, raises confidence to a much more significant plane and provides a more certain base (though not an absolute one) for action'. (1994: 3)

And they continue to argue for transparency in research processes:

> It is not just that we must somehow 'please' our critical colleague audiences; the deeper issue is avoiding self-delusion. After that we can turn to the task of being honest with our readers about how we did the study, and what worried us about its quality. Without such methodological frankness, we run the risk of reporting 'knowledge that ain't so'. (Ibid.: 294)

Different again in terms of scope is the requirement of Cohen, Manion and Morrison (2000: 73) that: 'Research design is governed by the notion of "fitness for purpose". The purposes of the research determine the methodology and design of the research.'

However, for all their differences, these and other definitions of methodology (see Appendix II) share a common idea of *justification*. This is why, in our own definition, we do not emphasise a conceptual essence for the term, but rather suggest an operational description which will be positively useful in justifying any given research design.

Traditionally, for philosophers the twin terms of methodology are ontology and epistemology, understood as the study of being and of knowing respectively. Basically, an ontology is a theory of what exists, and how it exists and an epistemology is a related theory of how we can come to know those things. For a philosopher these are specialist complex and profound fields of enquiry, but their importance is not restricted to philosophical enquiry, though their relevance at the point of setting out on an empirical research activity may not seem immediate.

Indeed, if every research thesis had to elaborate its ontological and epistemological background, then the wheel would truly be endlessly re-invented. However, if we examine any piece of empirical research, it is clear that there is at work a great many assumptions about what the world is, how it works and how we can claim to know these things.

Activity 2.5   What assumptions do you make?

In your research journal respond to these questions about the assumptions which underpin your study. (Clearly the extent to which you can respond to the following questions will depend on the stage you have reached in your own study.)

- What assumptions about the topic are inevitably present in the way I conceive of the study?
- What specific questions – in the light of my assumptions – am I asking in this particular study, and which events and circumstances prompted them and gave them a particular urgency?
- Why and how did these assumptions, questions and circumstances suggest or require the particular methods which I chose?
- What assumptions about 'how the world operates' – and how we can know it – are given with these methods?
- Why, then, are they particularly suitable for investigating the phenomena in question?
- How did the process of my research change or qualify my assumptions? In what ways am I changed by the research?
- And in what ways is the community's understanding changed by what I have achieved? If, as we are trying to suggest, research actually defines the field, what redefinition (however small) is suggested in my work?
- What might another researcher learn from my experience?

It is the task of methodology to uncover and justify research assumptions as far and as practicably as possible, and in so doing to locate the claims which the research makes within the traditions of enquiry which use it. Equally, it is our task, as researchers, to identify our research tools and our rationale for their selection.

We have developed our operational definition from our own work with research students who, in time-constrained studies for Higher degree awards, are not immediately concerned with the fine print of the epistemological and ontological foundations of their studies!

However, it is our experience that the really successful – that is, the *persuasive* – studies are those which demonstrate a clear, logical and reflexive relationship between research questions and field questions. Further, this relationship is not one which is articulated only or largely in a so-called 'methodology chapter', but one which is *evident throughout the work*. The relationship of research questions to literature review is a matter of methodology; the relationship of literature review to fieldwork is a methodological issue; the relationship of the fieldwork to the analysis of data is a methodological concern; the relationship of the framework for analysis to the research report is methodological.

> At the heart of all these interwoven research activities are endless processes of selection; and in constantly justifying this selection, a 'good methodology' is more *a critical design attitude* to be found always at work throughout a study, rather than confined within a brief chapter called 'Methodology'.

But what does this mean in practice? How might you work so that you were at all times *methodologically self-conscious*? We will discuss this further in Chapter 4.

So, what does it mean to adopt a *critical design attitude* in a research study? How does the *methodologically self-conscious researcher* behave? Our central concern is that student researchers are asked, not 'Have you done your Methodology chapter?' but 'What are the methodological structures and operations of your study?' In this sense research *is* methodology.

The operational definition of methodology which we discuss in this book can be summarised as having the following characteristics and strategies.

Methodology is . . .

'Methodology' is not something that is reported/accounted/'done with' in one chapter (though a version of it normally is).

'Methodology' starts on Day One.

'Methodology' irradiates the whole of the research.

'Methodology' is as much about choosing a tape-recorder as about reading Habermas.

'Methodology' *is* your research diary.

The whole research process is 'methodological', and this is evident in the 'persuasive' study.

Throughout the book we shall keep our operational definition to the forefront of our discussions. In the following section we explore further our definition of *methodology* by looking in particular at the relationship of *research questions* to those which are asked in empirical situations, and which we identify as *field questions*.

Why are research questions important?

It is important to distinguish between research questions – those that originate, shape and are to some extent answered by the study – from field questions – those that are actually put to people in whatever form.

In 2001 we asked 13 PhD students who had successfully framed and refined their research questions to talk about why they felt the formulation of research questions was an important early stage of their research act. All participants readily agreed that research questions were important and went on to explain why they mattered to their own studies. They wrote:

- My questions matter because they set the parameters for my study.
- These questions matter for me because they define the issues pertinent to my research, will help me to clarify the situation and find ways forward.
- My research questions set out the principles that the study is based on.
- These questions matter because it gives my research a clear focus. It is important that the research I do benefits others and not just me, and it is important that I know why I am doing the study.
- For me, it is important to return to such questions during the research process – to remember what I'm doing and why!
- Research should be enjoyable for the researcher, so the research topic is important to me. My particular research questions help me to clarify, and therefore justify, my own work and to work out the reasonings for doing it.

- These particular research questions are important in the clarification and development of the practical aspects of research.
- My research questions help focus attention on the more important aspects of writing up the study.
- They [the research questions] enable me to clarify thoughts about underlying reasons for the study I've chosen to carry out.
- The research questions are important because they are firstly important to me – they help me to be clear about what's important in what I'm doing.
- They are important in helping me to develop good research practice.
- The formulation of these questions has helped me to be clear in my thoughts and they give my research direction.
- Developing my research questions and then sticking closely to them in designing the small-scale study has kept my study going in the right direction.

Activity 2.6

Whether you have decided on your own research questions or whether you are still deciding on the precise form of words, look over the comments made by research students above and note down the responses which fit, in some way, your own feelings about your research questions.

Note the key words and phrases that occur in several different responses. Ask yourself, whether it is appropriate for you to include such terms in your own discussion of the importance of research questions.

The themes emerging from the responses of our students can be grouped into three categories: defining limits, clarification and empirical issues.

Research questions require researchers to:

- define the limits of their study
- clarify their research study
- identify empirical issues and work on empirical questions.

Generating and justifying research questions

In our own work we have developed two simple tools that can be employed in the generation of research questions: the 'Russian doll' principle and the 'Goldilocks test'. Applying the Russian doll principle means breaking down the research question from the original statement to something which strips away the complication of layers and obscurities until the very essence – the heart – of the question can be expressed. This may well mean phrasing and rephrasing the question so that each time its focus becomes sharpened and more defined – just as a Russian doll is taken apart to reveal finally a tiny doll at the centre.

The generated questions can then be subjected to the 'Goldilocks test' – a metaphor for thinking through the suitability of the research questions for a particular researcher in a particular setting at a particular time. So, we can ask: is this question 'too big', such that it cannot be tackled in this particular study at this time – perhaps it is a study which needs significant research funding or assistance which is not usually available to students doing research for an academic award? We can ask 'Is this too small?' – perhaps there is not enough substance to the question to warrant investigation. We can ask if the question is 'too hot' – perhaps an issue which is so sensitive that the timing is not right for investigation – or such that researching it at this point would be not only difficult but damaging in the particular social context. These questions will enable us finally to identify those questions which might be 'just right' for investigation at *this* time, by *this* researcher in *this* setting.

The following example will illustrate the application of the 'Russian doll' principle and the 'Goldilocks test'.

Case Sketch 2.1   Crowsfoot School

Crowsfoot School is a large comprehensive school in the South of England. Over the years several schools for pupils with special educational needs in the region have attempted to transfer pupils with learning difficulties into the school. Inclusion has worked for some pupils but not for all. Following the failure, recently, to include three pupils in succession, the head teacher asked for a review of the situation. She wanted to know what was working against the inclusion of pupils and if there was anything which could be done to improve the inclusion success rate at the school.

You visit the school to discuss the research study you have been commissioned to do. The head teacher gives you details of pupils whom the school has attempted to include in the past three years, and contact details for three 'feeder' special schools. You are given a tour of the school, meet the SENCO and have coffee in the staffroom at break time where you are introduced to staff who are taking their break there. Staffroom 'chat' indicates that there are a number of issues about which some staff are unhappy – there is no whole staff consensus or commitment to the 'inclusive' policy.

What research questions would guide such a study? Below are several alternatives, generated by students in a research questions workshop in response to the 'Crowsfoot' scenario.

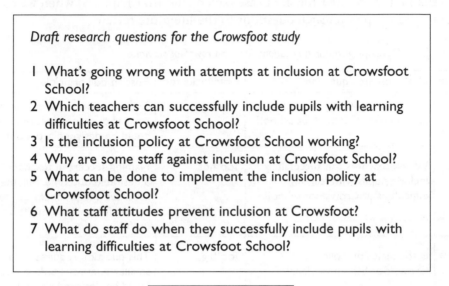

Draft research questions for the Crowsfoot study

1 What's going wrong with attempts at inclusion at Crowsfoot School?
2 Which teachers can successfully include pupils with learning difficulties at Crowsfoot School?
3 Is the inclusion policy at Crowsfoot School working?
4 Why are some staff against inclusion at Crowsfoot School?
5 What can be done to implement the inclusion policy at Crowsfoot School?
6 What staff attitudes prevent inclusion at Crowsfoot?
7 What do staff do when they successfully include pupils with learning difficulties at Crowsfoot School?

Activity 2.7

Apply the 'Goldilocks test' to research questions:

● Are any of the above questions too large, too small, too 'hot' ...

One way of refining research questions and applying the Goldilocks test and the Russian doll principle is to write the questions in order and, next to each question, decide on its 'Goldilocks' status and draw out any factors which will help you to refine the questions. Table 2.1 shows what our students did with the Crowsfoot questions.

This process suggests that questions 6: 'What staff attitudes prevent inclusion at Crowsfoot?' and 7: 'What do staff do when they successfully include pupils with learning difficulties at Crowsfoot school?' are the most appropriate beginnings for the study. Other questions (such as questions 2 and 4) indicate that the attitudes and practices of staff are key to providing responses to the head teacher's concerns about inclusion.

Finally, after thinking about the 'Russian doll' principle and the 'Goldilocks test' the students agreed on two questions for this study, designed to refine the focus of the research and to enable to effective generation of future empirical questions:

● To what extent do the attitudes of staff affect the inclusion of children with learning difficulties in Crowsfoot School?

- What steps might be taken to develop more inclusive attitudes and practices at Crowsfoot?

We shall return to the Crowsfoot case sketch later (in Chapter 5) when we consider the relationship of research questions to the literature review.

Table 2.1   *Developing research questions for the Crowsfoot scenario*

No.	Draft research question	Goldilocks test	Russian doll principle
1	What's going wrong with attempts at inclusion at Crowsfoot school?	Too big	This question requires several smaller questions before a study could be designed around it
2	Which teachers can successfully include pupils with learning difficulties at Crowsfoot school?	Too hot	Naming successful teachers is not a desirable outcome. But the attitudes and practices of successful teachers might be useful
3	Is the inclusion policy at Crowsfoot School working?	Too big	This question requires several smaller questions before a study could be designed around it
4	Why are some staff against inclusion at Crowsfoot School?	Too big (and perhaps too hot)	This question suggests that there might be a need to investigate staff attitudes
5	What can be done to implement the inclusion policy at Crowsfoot School?	Too big	This question points to the need to identify strategies for action
6	What staff attitudes prevent inclusion at Crowsfoot?	Just right?	Perhaps should be more clearly expressed
7	What do staff do when they successfully include pupils with learning difficulties at Crowsfoot School?	Just right?	This question will help to identify successful inclusive practices

Activity 2.8

Table 2.1 offers a strategy which you might use to support the development of your own research questions. When you are ready to do so, we suggest that you photocopy the blank version of Table 2.2 and use it to generate and refine your own research questions.

Table 2.2 *Framework for refining research questions*

No.	Draft research question	Goldilocks test	Russian doll principle
1			
2			
3			
4			
5			

What we have tried to emphasise in this chapter is the pervasive nature of methodology and the importance of framing questions which inform the creation of research methods. We shall return to these themes later.

The methodology of any study is unlikely to be complete until the research is arrested for the purposes of report; a methodology worthy of the name will be continuously and reflexively developed as the study proceeds – in much the same way as the data which emerge from methods reflect back on and qualify the suitability of those methods for the purpose in hand.

Endnote

Narrowly understood, a research methodology is sometimes seen as standing slightly outside of the main achievement of a study, a sort of guarantee – in the common sense of the term – whose small print may be technically necessary but hardly essential reading for the operation of the product! What we argue here, however, is a broader view of methodology as the very seat of justification of any claims which might follow. Methods mediate between research questions and the answers which data partially provide to them; methodology justifies and guarantees that process of mediation. In the end, the characteristic task for a methodology is to persuade the reader of the *unavoidably* triangular connection between *these* research questions, *these* methods used to operationalise them and *these* data so generated.

Activity 2.9

Before you leave this chapter, think about your own research study. Ask yourself:

Why are you doing this study in this way?
Can you justify the research decisions you have made?

Make some notes about the justification of your research design in your research journal.

CHAPTER SUMMARY

In this chapter we have:

Provided an overview of what we mean by methodology

Discussed the distinction between 'methods' and 'methodology'

Discussed, with examples, the function of methodological consideration in the context of your research study

Discussed the function and importance of research questions
Provided a structure within which you might generate and justify your research questions

Encouraged you to express, in writing, your own positions on the key elements of the chapter in relation to your research questions and methodology

📖 FURTHER READING

De Vaus, D. (2001) *Research Design in Social Research.*
London: Sage.

For a succinct summary of the importance of clarifying research questions and their operational and conceptual definitions read 'Tools for Research Design' (Chapter 2). This chapter focuses on the clarification of research questions and concepts at the outset of a study.

Halpin, D. and Troyna, B. (1994) *Researching Education Policy: Ethical and Methodological Issues.* London: Falmer.

A set of papers focusing on ethical and methodological concerns in researching educational policy – includes some examples of research studies.

PART 2

The Pervasive Nature
of Methodology

Looking: Seeing Beyond the Known

LEARNING OBJECTIVES

By studying and doing the activities in this chapter you will:

◇ develop an awareness of the importance of radical looking at all points during the research process

◇ have an understanding of the strategies which can be used in research involving different ways of seeing

◇ have studied two examples of research which demonstrate different dimensions of 'radical looking'

Introduction

> What we mean by radical looking is exploration *beyond the*
> *familiar* and the (personally) known, to the roots of a situation:
> this is exploration which makes the familiar strange.

If we travel to a different country we see everyday things in a new light and sometimes find ourselves becoming curious about the ordinary: traffic systems, shopping, eating, dress codes and other routines of life can be sources of fascination
because – although we *recognise* them – we do not fully understand them nor do we
know precisely how we should behave within the nuances of that *particular* society.
Travel, in effect, offers us the opportunity to hold our own experiences up to the
light and reflect on how we do things in the context of another culture. *Radical looking* can, in effect, involve the researcher in the role of *traveller* with curiosity about
the systems, cultures, practices and policies of the life of the setting in which she
has decided to work.

To give a quite literal example of this, Nutbrown (2001) reports the experience of
looking *outside* the UK provision for early childhood education. This offered an
opportunity to reflect again on more familiar contexts, in a report of her experience
of visiting some Italian pre-schools she wrote:

> Visiting any early childhood setting is a privilege, such was the case in visit-
> ing the Reggio Emilia Pre-schools. Pedagogistas, Atiliaristas, parents and chil-
> dren allowed us to witness their work and to discuss with them the intricacies
> of their thinking which led to the kinds of practices which were compelling
> and meaningful. Observations of course are so personal, and interpretation of
> what is seen depends upon the eyes through which those observations are
> made. This account is therefore a reflection of my own experience of those
> encounters; my own construction of Reggio 'as I saw it' .

Mirrors
There are mirrors everywhere in the Reggio centres. They fill large corners of
rooms, they hang from the ceiling, and they dangle in small fragments from
mobiles made by the children. They encourage looking, looking at oneself,
they make for reflection – and in some cases multi reflections of the same
image through mirror after mirror after mirror. The opportunity of so many
mirrors invites reflection; reflection on oneself, one's work and one's own
observations and assumptions.

Through the mirrors of Reggio Emilia centres I saw much that I recognised,
much that makes sense in terms of what I believe is 'right' for children, I saw
many of my own values, and many of my principles in practice. I saw too, so

much of the excellence of teaching young children that can also be seen in many nurseries and early childhood centres in the UK. (Nutbrown, 2001: 120–22)

This extract illustrates our point that looking at others can help us to reflect on our own experiences. Simultaneously, historical reflection can enable us to look back at the events of the past (Anning, 1997; Bruce, et al. 1995; McCulloch and Richardson, 2001). We can also 'dig' into the 'objects' of research settings (much as an archaeologist might do) and thus uncover clues which we then piece together to help us to understand circumstances and policy contexts of the context of study. In these ways all social and educational researchers are historians and archaeologists, aiming to understand origins and contexts of the situations they study.

Radical looking, then, requires that researchers develop the skills of travellers and historians in so far as they look at events close to them *as if* they were different or distant.

Making the familiar strange

All researchers need to develop the capacity to see their topic with *new and different lenses*, in order to look beyond and transform their own current knowledge. Topics present themselves for research in different ways, and for all sorts of different reasons. What distinguishes research from everyday interest or curiosity, however, is the *opening up of familiar things to alternative ways of seeing*.

Two groups of people often studied in social science research are children and the disabled. But it is only relatively recently that children and disabled people have become participants rather than 'objects' of research; it is only recently that their voices have been heard. In Chapter 2 we suggested that an *interest* in a subject only starts to become *research* when a curiosity is systematically informed by perspectives outside of the researcher's normal vision. This means asking questions about what is already known, what previous research has been done, what policy contexts affect the situation and what the participants themselves think about their present position. In asking such questions the researcher engages in *radical looking at others' knowledge*. Responses to such questions refine and define the topic. The process involves the researcher in examining, and either incorporating or rejecting information as s/he begins to focus on a particular problem, a particular gap in knowledge.

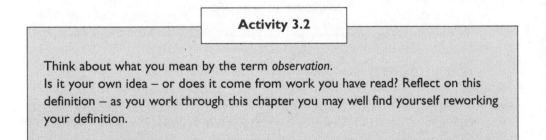

Activity 3.1   Making the familiar strange

Try this task.

Imagine you are a cleaner in the institution or organisation where you work. Describe how the organisation looks, how it works, from your viewpoint.

Seeing things from the point of view of someone else, who occupies a different role, gives an indication of what we mean by adopting a research stance which involves radical looking, the *opening up of familiar things to alternative ways of seeing.*

In the next two sections we provide two examples from our own research to demonstrate aspects of radical looking and interpret the theme first in terms of observation and, second, in reflective responses to data and their analyses.

Observation in research

Although observations are often referred to in terms of particular techniques, what we want to attend to here is the nature of looking. Our working definition of observation here is simply 'looking' – looking critically, looking openly, looking sometimes knowing what we are looking for, looking for evidence, looking to be persuaded, looking for information.

In this section we shall point you to some ideas about, and methods of, observation and draw on a research report which used observations of one child, Alex, during her first five years.

Activity 3.2

Think about what you mean by the term *observation.*

Is it your own idea – or does it come from work you have read? Reflect on this definition – as you work through this chapter you may well find yourself reworking your definition.

Below is a list of different ways of looking or observing. Different techniques will be useful for different settings and you will need to consider the ethics, practicalities, and justification of each of those you choose to use.

- checklists
- structured observations with a schedule
- time sampling

- mapping
- target pupil observations
- video and photographic records
- unstructured observations
- one-way mirror observations.

These techniques are discussed in several texts on research methods (see Appendix H). The main issue is to be clear about what you want to research and why, and then find the best way of working on your research question.

Observation is a widely used research method and perhaps all too easily undertaken. Some early questions will help to justify the decision to use this method: what is the purpose of the observation? What is the focus of the observation? What data gathering methods will best serve the purpose? How will the data be used?

Activity 3.3   Making observations

Beginning their section on observation (chapter 17) Cohen, Manion and Morrison write:

> Observational data are attractive as they afford the researcher the opportunity to gather 'live' data from 'live' situations. The researcher is given the opportunity to look at what is taking place *in situ* rather than at second hand (Patton 1990). This enables researchers to understand the context of programmes, to be open-ended and inductive, to see things that might otherwise be unconsciously missed, to discover things that participants might not freely talk about in interview situations, to move beyond perception-based data (e.g. opinions in interviews), and to access personal knowledge. Because observed incidents are less predictable there is a certain freshness to this form of data collection that is denied in other forms, e.g. questionnaire or a test. (Cohen, Manion and Morrison, 2000: 305)

In your research journal identify three advantages and three drawbacks of using observation techniques to gather data in your research study.

Observing Alex

Nutbrown (1999) used observations in a study of one child's literacy development. Observations were made using different techniques at different times over a period of five years. This kind of ethnographic study involved parents of the child noting literacy events, use of home videotapes as well as direct observations at different points in time. These unstructured observations were the main source of data.

In the report which follows, an account of behaviour is given within a whole social context where observations were made as the opportunity presented itself rather than at predetermined times or for specific lengths of time intervals. The purpose was not to *intervene*, simply to *understand*.

The careful recording of observations throughout the study was essential for accuracy and chronology. Some observations were very short, others longer, but the context was always noted as well as the particular literacy event. One task was to generate data that would make it possible to tell a story of one child's literacy learning, but equally important was the job of finding ways to analyse, interpret and ultimately report the data. Reporting observational data can pose problems. It is important to tell the story, but giving a blow by blow account can be over-lengthy, dull for the reader and sometimes difficult to make sense of. One job of the research report is to 'clear the clutter' and get to the heart of the issues. In the example which follows it was a case of turning a bank of observations made over several years into an accessible report that people who were not present at the real events could become part of, engage with and bring their own meaning to. In the following account of Alex's early literacy development, the observations were, with some ruthlessness, selected and sorted to tell a chronological story.

Learning about literacy in the earliest years
ALEX AT HOME

Among the gifts given to Alex when she was born were books. They included: *The Jolly Postman*; *Fairy Letters*; *Old Bear*; *Peekaboo*; *Bouncing*; *The Children's Illustrated Bible*. At three months of age she was used to being sung nursery rhymes whilst being bounced on her grandmother's knee, and one of her favourite toys was a foam-fabric covered brick printed with **A B C** and pictures of an apple, a ball and a cat, corresponding to the letters. She enjoyed small books read to her whilst she lay on her back on her rug, and she began to handle the books, similarly to her handling of other objects which she encountered in her world, so exploring their qualities – finding out how they felt and how they behaved to her touch.

Alex's bedroom curtains were printed with letters of the alphabet as was her cot cover. Nursery rhyme tapes were played in the car – a regular accompaniment on journeys as she travelled in her car seat looking out on an ever changing environment of print on advertising hoardings, in shop windows and on street signs. Some of Alex's clothes were embroidered with logos, letters and captions, such as: *Baby, ABC, I love my Daddy, super tot, Sweater Shop!, Good Morning Sunshine!*, and *Who loves you baby?* Alex enjoyed a baby book of padded cloth pages, printed with simple pictures and single words, she sucked it, gnawed it, pulled it, fingered it and gazed at it.

By five months Alex held small books for herself, chewed them, and made her own baby babbling noises as she gazed at the illustrations. At six months regular visits to the swimming pool meant new encounters with print, and at eight months she sat at the piano on her uncle's knee whilst he played Scott Joplin with the sheet music propped up on the music stand in front. At eight months too, she enjoyed emptying a cloth bag printed with the words **My Books**, and explored the miniature, hard cover books which the bag contained. As she lay on her back or her tummy looking at the pages 'talking' to the children she saw on the pages, she sucked the covers, turned the pages and rotated the books over and over in her hands. She delighted herself as characters in a small pop up book sprang from the page as she opened it, and having discovered the phenomena she repeated the actions again and again. At this age, having stories read was a familiar and regular pleasure. Sitting on a large floor cushion exploring the holes in *Peepo* was a favourite choice at nine months, fingering the holes and turning the pages seemed such a comfortable way to spend time, and her commentary of shrieks and babbling to accompany the pictures confirmed her interest and enjoyment. Pages turned, sometimes by accident, sometimes seemingly by design, but books were explored with thoroughness and diligence, as were building bricks, stacking towers, cuddly toys and all household objects and people within easy grasp.

By nine months of age Alex was familiar with the actions of Pat-a-cake – and raised her hands as her mother completed the rhyme with '*Toss it up high!*' And at 10 months she used household bottles with printed letters and logos in her bath and paddling pool, and played with empty boxes and bags – each printed with colourful arrangements of words and pictures. Enjoyable too, at 10 months was rummaging through the pages of a newspaper spread on the floor, ripping and tearing the pages covered in print of different fonts and sizes. 'Joining in' whilst her parents wrote on the word processor, by tapping at the keys she created on the screen:

> dvhulwefhu fcff 9 w 9f 9 8 4 v I fiwiooqaopfgr0g \
> we
> =9t00g w0-wt ki d 2e7u0942908480948y,.tt48-y 9y y ,
> ,##9h-9y90,y,h,. h,..
> mmmmmmmmmmmmmmmmmmmmmmmmmmmmmmmmmmmm
> mmmmmmmmmmmmmmmmmmmmmmmmmmmmmmmmmmmm
> mmmmmmmmmmmmmmmmmmmmmmmmmmmvuyf
> yuvfkbguougy878b

Her tapping on the keys produced visual feedback, similar tapping whilst sitting on her father's lap at the electronic keyboard to sing nursery rhymes produced the feedback of sound with the visual symbols of music already static in front of her on the music stand.

When she was 11 months old, Alex learned to start her tape player (a model with large colourful controls designed for young children to use), and she seemed content to let nursery rhyme and story tapes wash over her while she played. She also flipped through colourful magazines found on the floor – in much the same casual way as some adults in a doctors waiting room!

It was just before her first birthday that Alex received her first felt tipped pens, these washable sticks of colour were first chewed, resulting in a mouth gloriously coloured red, turquoise and purple. Given paper, the first marks she made appeared accidental, it seemed she did not know what the pens would do. Why would she? It was her first experience of using a tool to make marks on paper. The nearest she had come to such objects before had turned out to be edible – sticks of bread or carrot. Her closest mark making experience was tracing her fingers through a pool of yoghurt tipped onto the tray at her high chair seat. Random marks made by the bright felt tip colours gradually evolved during her second year with practice and developing strength and control she moved from making light and sometimes accidental marks to gaining control of the pens and making them produce back and forth lines of different colours.

Book reading continued and the 18 month old Alex enjoyed borrowing books from the library, playing with the climbing frame in the children's area of the library and sitting on the bean bags listening to stories. She began to receive postcards as well, from her grandmother who lived some miles away. Each card was greeted with sheer delight, and Alex began to collect the post from the doormat each morning, always pleased when there was something for her. She posted her cards through various slots, including the video recorder and the letter box in the front door – from inside to the outside! – playing her own game of sending and receiving cards through the letterbox.

Alex saw her parents using literacy at home: writing notes; doing domestic paper-work; checking the bank statement; writing birthday cards; reading the paper; doing the crossword; jotting a note (or doodling) during a telephone conversation; writing a shopping list; using a word processor; reading the television listings; marking a date on the kitchen calendar.

Literacy was in evidence when Alex celebrated her second birthday. She was accustomed to receiving post, and so keenly and competently ripped open envelopes containing birthday cards, the messages and names of senders being read to her. This was a skill she had rehearsed to a fine art when her baby brother was born. Alex was aged two years and nine months at the time and so opened some of the many cards sent to congratulate the family on Ben's birth. She also wrote her own little messages to the baby, using yellow 'post-it' labels and stuck them – in plenty – on his cot. She read some of her books to him, using different voices for different characters – and repeating a particularly enthralling rendition of *The three bears* – with voices of different pitch for Father Bear and Mother Bear and an especially tiny and high pitched tone for Baby Bear. This telling of a familiar story bore much resemblance to the way her mother told the story – time and time again – with Alex, enthralled – sitting on her lap. Perhaps Alex wanted to give her baby brother the same pleasure, perhaps she just enjoyed having a captive audience for her story-telling. Whatever the reason, '*Goldifox*' always escaped just in time and was '*neffer seeda gen!*'

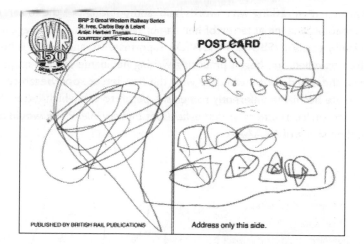

Alex's enjoyment of books grew as she reached her third birthday, she loved to read familiar pop-up books and traditional tales to herself – in her own way, telling her own versions of the stories and paying close attention to the illustrations for clues to the plot. She enjoyed books such as *Spot*, *Dear Zoo*, and *My presents*. Finding the repetition a pleasure, perhaps a necessity, and delighting in lifting each flap and gasping with feigned surprise each time she 'discovered' what was beneath each flap. At bedtime, however, she seemed to like to lie and listen to longer stories, so her parents began by reading their own favourite, *The House at Pooh Corner*. The volume was read and read from beginning to end, over many nights, Alex falling asleep whilst *Pooh, Tigger, Eeyore and friends* played out their days with Christopher Robin in the Hundred Acre Wood. Once the last chapter was read it was time to begin again. Alex enjoyed bedtime listening to poems and rhymes and other 'classic' children's literature, *Alice's Adventures in Wonderland*, *The Borrowers*, *The Tales of Beatrix Potter* (even though she was never quite sure how to say soporific), the *Just So Stories* and *Paddington Bear*. Initially Alex's mother thought these stories too complex, reading such stories to a young child smacked of 'force feeding', went against the grain of what the books about 'reading to your child' said about literature for young children. *Alice in Wonderland* did not feature in the list of books suitable for Under Fives which her mother picked up at the local library. But here perhaps is a difference between home and school, between literacy happenings in families and literacy curriculum in school. At home there are no 'set texts', no written 'rules' about what it is right to read, at home it is OK to try it and see, at home it is fine to read what you enjoy. So the more complex texts, the well established childhood classics, some published 100 years before Alex was born were included in her repertoire, because, at home, it *felt* like the right thing to do simply because Alex enjoyed listening to the words wash over her at bedtime.

The foundations of enjoying books and understanding how they worked were well laid (and continued to be built upon) during the year in which Alex became four, and in that year too she seemed to consolidate her understanding of signs and symbols in the environment, asking what words 'said' and pointing out the letters she recognised, especially the initial letter of her name; ever present in the registration plate of the family car, SAINSBURY'S and ASDA supermarkets, and the 94A bus on which she often travelled. She began practising writing her name in earnest just after her fourth birthday and content initially with the first letter, soon began to notice that adults wrote her name differently to her, she began to ask which letters 'came next' and insisted on 'correctness' *Is that right? Does that say 'Alex'?* she would ask producing another string of AAAAAA.

Alex was a collector; of print, words, books and letters. She collected words with a voracious appetite, seeking any handy pen and paper to write down another word from a box or label which she came across – such as *Dalmatians* from her Disney video and 'ECONOMY' copied from the bottle of fabric conditioner left on the floor at the side of the washing machine.

Alex's early years (and those of her baby brother) were filled with literacy. They were rich in other things too and it is important that an account such as this, which takes a particular focus, does not forget that the child who read, wrote and learned many nursery rhymes also dug up worms in the garden, shrieked with joy as she splashed water in her paddling pool, hurt her knees and needed cuddles when she fell off her bike, left her toys in a trail behind her and hated cleaning her teeth! There was a balance to living and learning, and literacy was part of the balance of opportunities, experiences and challenges in her early years. (Nutbrown, 1999: 95–107)

Activity 3.4

Thinking about the report of the study you have just read, try to identify the ways in which '*the familiar was made strange*' in order to provide the account.

What are you looking *for?*

Radical looking means much more than using observations to generate data for a research study.

> *Radical looking* holds within it the important dimension of looking *for* as well as looking *at*, the act of seeking *meanings* as well as *evidence*.

The following paper provides an example of what we mean by looking *for* and demonstrates how *meanings* are generates in response to the act of radical looking *through* data to see the truths they hold.

Exclusive tendencies: concepts, consciousness and curriculum in the project of inclusion

PETER CLOUGH

This paper explores a view that exclusive structures in institutions reflect exclusive structures in the development of consciousness. In the context of a current rhetoric of inclusion in the UK, the paper starts by examining some of the theoretical conditioners of policy and practice in Special Educational Needs, and hence their effects on teacher thinking. Drawing on a survey of teacher perspectives on SEN, the paper identifies their correlation with economic resources, but asks whether exclusive attitudes might be further explained in terms of conceptual development. The paper thus brings together argument from (variously empirical) psychological, sociological and philosophical enquiry to question assumptions about the moral and political project of inclusion.

Introduction

This paper outlines and examines an argument which is, at once, very much of the age and (perhaps, therefore, also) morally and politically suspect. The argument has a prima-facie simplicity: we have exclusive structures in our institutions because those same structures organize consciousness; little wonder that our schools and our curricula *include* some at the same defining moment as they *exclude* others, when the very process by which individual identity is formed is just such a selective and ultimately discriminatory affair. Now such a constructionist point of view could be seen as a journalistic – if not omnibus – truism were it not for the fact that a major-ity of calls for inclusive educational systems take for granted their moral necessity without proper regard for the very political conditions that mediate their *emotional* acceptability. So we might wonder whether an inclusive philosophy is not only naive, but also dishonest, because it assumes what it seeks to establish; that is, that inclu-sion is morally necessitated and *structurally* indicated: get the structures right, one might say, and humanity will follow. However, it cannot be assumed that inclusion is a simple 'given' of natural life, a necessary property of consciousness or culture (or, therefore, of the curricula which mediate them). Indeed, exclusion may be necessar-ily as much at the centre of consciousness and social structure as inclusion, so that the argument for inclusive education is a much more complex matter than is con-tained in the belief that a naturally inclusive mind is hindered from its true moral expression in socially inclusive structures.

The discussion which follows will:

- characterize the current state of special/inclusive education in the UK;
- rehearse the historical/theoretical precedents of that state;
- examine the role of teachers in those realizations;
- report an investigation of teachers' perspectives on SEN;
- sketch a framework for understanding exclusion as a function of consciousness.

Recent developments in UK special education

The changes which have affected education in the UK in recent years have been the more remarkable in special education. These include:

- the increasingly explicit politicization of educational structures and processes;
- the wide- and deep-ranging development of legislation which increases the regulation and control of education through central policies;
- at the same time as this, the development of certain areas of responsibility (most importantly, funding) to schools;
- the consequent 'marketization' of schooling, and the increasing separation, both within schools and in the broader institutions which maintain them, of managers from professionals;

● the development of an accountability ethos which effectively promotes instru-
mentalism within the curriculum.

All such changes are in fact all the more noticeable in special schooling, since its
regulation notably in general was traditionally – and sometimes notoriously – open
to local and hence widely varying interpretation. Thus, the basis on which decisions
were made about appropriate schooling for those with learning difficulties could
vary tremendously from one local education authority (LEA) to the next, according
to the traditions of practice which had determined a certain pattern of provision; as
has often been noted – and as is borne out by government statistics – whether
children with learning difficulties attend special schools or not may depend more on
where they live than on their learning needs (Swann 1989).

An even more noticeable change, however, is in the area of the curriculum. In the
old dispensation, the greater part of what went on in special schooling was a matter for schools – and frequently individual teachers – to decide; the curriculum could
be as arbitrary as were many of the decisions which had led to a child's particular
placement. Now, of course, a statutory National Curriculum in the UK affects – if
only by technical default – the education of all learners, and the degrees of freedom
open to teachers in their selection of curricula are considerably more limited.

Perhaps the greatest change, however, is in the culture of special schooling. Effectively as cultures unto themselves, special schools and 'special' departments in mainstream schools were distinctive by nature of a broadly deficit-centred ideology
which – relatively unhindered by regulation – could issue in practices accountable to
a notion of individual pathology (Golby and Gulliver 1979). To be sure, there were
poor or obviously 'bad' practices which did little to extend either the children themselves or any cause of difficulty; indeed, the curricula on offer could vary in precisely
these terms between the extremes of daily, sometimes quixotic and situation-sensi-
tive improvisation in some settings to the rigour of an instrumental learning form
organized by an often poorly – though surely benignly – understood behaviourist
psychology. In any event, teaching intentions were regulated – and mediated – more
by implicit traditions of professional practice and personal preference than by any
explicit, mandatory and essentially externally imposed requirement. The introduction
of statutory funding, curricular and assessment frameworks brings this culture of
child-centred education to a crisis, since the organizing principle of management
becomes one of accountability to structures hierarchically far removed from the
immediate and daily needs of any child (though they are surely *intended* to guarantee the meeting of such needs).

Old wine in new bottles?

How radical are these changes beyond the phenomena of structure? How do they
affect, for example, the degrees to which teachers will embrace instances of learning

difficulty and inclusive processes? Can these changes ever seriously erode an arguably fundamental principle and purpose of special provision, as claimed, for example, by Dessent (as long ago as 1983, but enduringly characteristic):

> Whatever else special education [in mainstream or segregated provision] involves, it is first and foremost an administrative and organisational system whereby one group of professionals are invested with responsibility for handicapped and 'difficult-to-teach' children. At the same time, other groups are absolved from such responsibility . . . [Special educational *historical roots lie in the need to remove responsibility for teaching children with SEN from teachers in normal schools.* (Dessent 1983; emphasis added)

I should suggest that these roots are still vigorous, however much academic re-conceptualizations of special education (as integrative or inclusive) may have rearranged the furniture of provision (Corbett 1998). For unless teachers in the UK opt during their initial training to teach children with learning difficulties, they do not expect to do so. Thus is created a culture of teachers with a tendency to exclude.

Let me briefly rehearse the spirit of the changes which the Warnock Report and subsequent Education Acts (DES 1981, 1988) pursued. At the centre of the Act was a view of learning difficulties as relative phenomena specific events tied to particular learning environments, rather than enduring conditions reflecting stable abilities and disabilities. The perceived source of difficulty is moved outside of the learner's head, as it were, to his or her learning environment, while action on those difficulties moves correspondingly from the child to the curriculum again which those difficulties are noticeable. As Wedell (1985) put this: 'The concept of special educational need is a relative one and need is seen as the outcome of the interaction between the resources and deficiencies of the child, and the resources and deficiencies of his [sic] environment.'

This leads to what might be called a curricular conception of learning difficulties. In this account:

> special educational needs are not noticed in a vacuum, as it were; they appear against a background of 'normal' ability and performance which gives them relief; they are noticed because the students fail to meet the requirements of a given curriculum. They are ways of locating and describing the points of mismatch between individual understanding and performance on the one hand, and the notional demands of a given curriculum on the other. They are inevitably norm-referenced, and the norms which give them their distinctness are in the first instance those of the given curriculum. However, we have not in the past typically admitted and considered this background; to be sure, the child's engagement with the curriculum tells us something about him or her, but it also tells us a great deal about the curriculum. Thus we have tended to reify a notional disability rather than attend to the broader and much more elusive curricular data of

which any given 'failing' is an abstraction. Let us say finally, then, that learning difficulties only occur in specific and describable contexts, though too often we generalise the difficulty and fail adequately to describe its context. (Clough 1998)

The date of this reference tells its own story but it has a logic and a rhetoric which
have struggled to survive the raft of political upheaval which has effectively changed
the very language of education (Corbett 1996). Such definitions – of curriculum and
learning difficulty – belong now to the privileged language of the academy, and would
be laughed out of most school staffrooms. Such a conceptualization was not, of
course, 'wrong', but it depended for its life on very different political (and hence
resource) fuels from those which drive education in the late 1990s. There is an
increasing return to popular (and, indeed, governmental) views of 'failure' (of individual students, teachers and, indeed, schools), low attainment, disaffection and non-
attendance as defects without meaning outside of the individuals concerned. In this
way, the signals of institutional failure can be muted, the experiences of the individuals marginalized and their 'difficulties' picked off with minimum tearing of the fabric
of the *status quo*.

Teachers making policy: policy making teachers?

It is in the nature of traditions that they evolve slowly, and that their features remain
in professional consciousness and practice long after their original bestowal of
meaning may have disappeared. (Cyril Burt, for example, may be academically dis-
credited, but the legacy of his work is ineradicable.) It is in the nature of traditions
that they may go along for the most part unreflectively and uncritically, but that it
takes vigorous, 'dewi-scale' and well-explicated revolution to overturn them. Is it
likely, then, that a new dispensation of inclusivity can seriously erode the *status quo*
of tradition which has its roots in much deeper structures of society than the simply educational?

In the end, it is teachers who mediate policy through their activities in and out of
the classroom, through their participation in the realization of curriculum. But in the
case of students with learning difficulties, this curriculum is still unavoidably infected
with notions of child-deficit. Through teacher education (as a function of a broader
academic tradition) psychology has imposed frameworks of interpretation which
have fundamentally conditioned teachers' understandings of what happens in their
classrooms and schools; psychology has elaborated categorical conceptions of personal, educational and social life which directly affect the decisions taken daily about
every child whose performance in the classroom is in any way remarkable.

The point is an important one if we are to understand how the present system
(of broadly exclusive provision) is supported not merely in the structures of society
(such as its institutions), but necessarily *in the structures of experience of the individuals
who participate in that culture.*

An illustration

What follows is an illustration of some of the ways in which recent SEN policy in the UK has directly affected school practices and teacher attitudes. In 1991, I carried out a survey of nearly 1000 mainstream teachers' perspectives on SEN, in 16 secondary schools divided equally among four English LEAS.[1] Several items in a lengthy questionnaire sought to explore the teachers' willingness to integrate children with various learning difficulties into their classrooms and schools; and, in particular, three separate though clearly conceptually related questions pursued their commitment to broad inclusivity; views on banding by 'ability'; professional commitment to teaching pupils with SEN.

Table 1 shows a collapse of these three items to indicate those teachers who answered unequivocally positively to three 'key' integrative/inclusive statements.

Table 1.   Percentage of teachers in agreement with all three 'key' statements (n 986)

	LEA1	LEA2	LEA3	LEA4
Teacher who said: 'All or most students with special educational needs should be educated in mainstream' *and* 'I would NOT like banding by ability' *and* 'I am happy that my job involves teaching ALL pupils'	15	23	47	30

Even before statistical sophistication, it is clear that something special is happening here, as revealed by the LEA3 scores (and a fuller, critical account is given elsewhere).[2] For the purposes of this paper, however, I wish merely to emphasize here that each of the LEAs had explicitly articulated integration policies; that each had – variously within the five years previous to my survey – undertaken some extra SEN-focused initiative; that each had an elected, advisory and administrative staff wholly committed to integrative principles; and that, by and large, the pattern of institutional distribution of students with SEN was common throughout the four LEAS. How, then, do we explain the LEA3 responses (which, in their tenor, were consistent throughout the whole of the questionnaire's 45 central items)?

Crudely it can be said that what chiefly distinguished LEA3 from the other LEAs was that it put its money (and considerably more of it) where its mouth was, and while all LEAs demonstrated vigorously written and stated policies, those of LEA3 were more transparently enacted. Resources were visibly and considerably attached to the development of supportive structures, *for both students and staff*; importantly, these included not only relatively generous staffing of in-school and out-school support teams, but the promotion – through financial inducements – of a broader bedrock of structures, continuous with an integrative principle (such as mixed-ability teaching across the curriculum).

Part of this study was replicated in 1997 (Jones 1998). The 1991 questionnaire – with some additional questions – was administered to all the staff of the four schools of LEA3. From a methodological point of view, there are certain variables, with variable impurity, which are currently under analysis; these include:

- changes in national and local policy (between 1991 and 1997) (arguably the most 'pure' basis of comparison);
- changes in governmental status of some of the schools studied;
- changes in establishment personnel in each of the schools studied (probably the most 'impure' variable).

In respect of each of these suites of changes, most significantly:

- aspects of the Education Act 1988 have been enacted and developed; and, more particularly, the Code of Practice (1996) has been introduced;
- two of the LEA3 schools studied – Schools 2 and 3 (see table 2) – have obtained grant maintained status;[3]
- personnel in the four LEA3 schools has changed (though only by some 8.4% over all the LEA schools).

Though the analysis of cross-tabulation of items given at table 1 is not yet available, there is currently salience (if not yet significance) to be found in the following: in the question which sought views on personal satisfaction with their own role in integrative teaching systems, respondents were asked to affirm one of the following statements about their involvement in SEN work:

'I am sympathetic but feel that it is not really my job.'
'I accept that it is my job but wish that it wasn't.'
'I am happy that my job involves teaching all pupils.'

Responses were expressed as given in table 2.

Table 2. Responses to the question about personal/professional satisfaction with direct involvement with students with SEN: comparison of responses 1991 and 1997 in LEA3 schools

	School	(1991 n = 265; 1997 n – 225)	
		Percentage of teachers 1997	Percentage of teachers 1991
'I am happy that my job involves teaching ALL pupils'	1	86.1	73.3
	2	83.6	83.3
	3	82.4	81.2
	4	83	76.4

Clearly there was no significant erosion of stated positive teacher attitudes (to SEN) in the schools which had obtained GM status while changes in the other two schools' scores have some statistical significance (even allowing for changes in personnel). And, indeed, the research affirms that Schools 2 and 3 had been able to sustain their resourcing of a properly supported, integrative SEN support system, while Schools 1 and 4 had struggled to maintain an integrative system without adequate resourcing: little wonder, then, that roughly a quarter of each school's staff was effectively challenging the idea of integration.

Discussion

All of these phenomena will be familiar in their generality; there is nothing remarkable here and it appears to be true – if a truism – that resources can buy attitudes; the corollary, of course, is that positive attitudes can atrophy in keeping with the shrinking of resources. It is thus possible to explain this in economic terms but it might be asked: what is at work beyond the mere economic explanation of this movement? For I would argue that the economic explanation takes for granted – without explicitly mentioning it – the structure of consciousness which allows that explanation. So, yes – resources operate causally and differentially on attitudes, but what is it in human experience which not only permits but effectively structures that relationship? Quite how in experience do resources correlate with teacher attitudes, conceptualizations and practices?

Three concepts of inclusiveness

At the beginning of this paper, I characterized some of the features of both the psychometric and sociological approaches to learning difficulties. The arguments against the former are well-rehearsed (see e.g. Barton 1996), but critique of the other perspective less so. In particular, and in this context of argument about inclusion, sociological approaches appear to operate through the kind of critique and research which identifies difficulties in the path of inclusion, as though these were just obstacles to something that is natural and inarguably good. This is often accompanied by a rhetoric (of 'the struggle': Barton 1996) to support the political implementation of inclusion. Both this research and rhetoric derive from a perspective which assumes that social and mental structures are isomorphic, in the sense that a presumed naturally inclusive mind is hindered from its true, moral expression in socially inclusive structures by various imposed and immoral exclusive practices. This is in contrast, of course, to the opposing psychometric view that mind and society are intrinsically exclusive and competitive.

How might an analysis of the concepts of inclusion and exclusion allow us to advance beyond these positions, and define the research agenda in a new way? More specifically, we can ask what can we mean when we use these concepts? For there is a number of possible ways of forming and **using** concepts of inclusion and exclusion, and these depend upon particular understandings of concept formation and use. By way of conclusion, I shall outline three possible concepts of inclusiveness.

- The first is the traditional theory of abstraction, which states that concepts are formed through our identifying resemblances between things (Bolton 1972), and then generalizing from these to form classes. On this basis, the task of forming judgements about inclusion and exclusion is that of attending to real resemblances and differences between people, and placing them inside or outside classes. These judgements are based upon inspection of data and, consequently, are of a universal nature (e.g. 'All children with such-and-such a Learning Difficulty should be . . .').

- The second view arises from a critique of the first. As Husserl (1901) pointed out, we would not generalize from one item to the next if we did not already possess some idea enabling us to see how items resemble one another. So, what is important in forming a concept is the application of a particular perspective or principle. In this case, the argument over inclusion/exclusion is about which principles are to be applied in order to group or separate individuals. This second perspective is commonly seen as supporting a pluralist and contextualist view (although there is no logical necessity in elevating pluralism to a universalist principle of inclusiveness).

- A third view is a synthesis of the first two. We can borrow from Hegel (1894) here, for there is a parallel between his doctrine of three mental functions and the foregoing description of the nature of concepts. The first function, which Hegel calls 'Understanding', is a conceptual activity which isolates and fixes boundaries. It places events in categories which are seen as independent, not requiring other ideas either for development or contrast. Then we have a second function called 'Dialectic proper', which opposes the separatist system of Understanding as absurd, as presupposing the things it excludes, for things cannot meaningfully be credited with the character given to them except in the setting provided by other seemingly external, seemingly irrelevant factors. Finally, the Hegelian dialectic posits a third function, which is called 'Reason' or 'Speculation', and whose purpose is to undo the neat isolation and fixation of the first thought function while, at the same time, preserving the distinctions which it has introduced. From this perspective, contextualization and categorization require each other as necessary parts of the same process. The sort of thinking required here is a long way from the dogmas of (psychometrically oriented) exclusion and the too-easy rhetoric of inclusiveness.

This is difficult work which does not issue in an obvious programme of research enquiry. I would suggest that what is broadly needed is much more close-order analysis of professional judgements in practice in various contexts; in this way, I suspect, we should see that there is really no prior definition and theory of inclusion/exclusion, since it is made and remade again and again – or not – in practice. As Wilson and Cowell (1984) have it:

> We have to find out what principles and assumptions control the thinking (and hence the decisions) of those concerned [with SEN] . . . For . . . the assumptions are often hidden, not only from the interviewer but from the person inter- viewed. Much time and effort is required to grasp the shape and style of a per- son's deepest thoughts. [And] in the case of handicap [sic] . . . it would be unwise to start from any particular view about identification and 'treatment'; we need rather . . . to map out the views and concepts of people in the business without any implication that they measure up, or fail to measure up to a preestablished picture . . .

Conclusion

Primarily and by definition, institutions exclude, cultures exclude and curricula exclude. Curricula have always been a means of exclusion; they have always been the means by which, ultimately, this group of students is separated from that. Decisions about 'ability' based on psychometric or other forms of assessment lead ultimately to decisions about what can and should be studied. Such decisions themselves reach deep into ideologies, for the curriculum is and always has been a selection from cul- ture for particular ends. Of course, this seems to be more glaringly the case with the introduction of the National Curriculum, but it is so in any culture in any time; what and whom we choose to teach are vital determinants of the part which those stu- dents are able to play in shaping a society's development.

In order to bring about a more truly inclusive schooling and society, we need to start from a recognition that exclusive principles are no less at the co-structured heart of 'organism and organization' (Williams 1965) than are inclusive intentions. We have to understand more about the ways in which inevitably limited resources may be correlated – sometimes quite subtly – with attitudes, and we have to find a way of understanding teachers' resistance to inclusive practice without pathologiz- ing, or even demonizing it. For the dynamics of such resistance are complex, and their occurrence is growing. Actually, the bulk of the empirical work which gave the above project its character derived from extensive life-historical exploration, and so these are the data which ultimately give some plausible life to a rational resistance. There may be in the margins of the profession a very small minority of teachers whose attitudes to exceptionality are vile, but they are not to be confused with that larger portion who struggle uncomfortably to articulate a growing resistance. The motif of resistance and of a tendency to exclude is more imaginatively captured by the words of Andrew, a teacher in the COSEN study and 44-year-old Head of History in a 1200 student 11–18 school:

'I don't have any difficulty with the kids like this [with SEN] . . . I mean I have no practical or . . . whatever, political difficulty with them in my classes . . . Well, I do have practical difficulties and that's the point, that *is* the point. I teach a subject [History] which is . . . finally non-negotiable in content, I mean in examinable content, and . . . I suppose in the way it has to be learned. And taught. So if I'm going to succeed . . . personally, that is, and professionally and if the school's going to succeed in the [local press], I've got to go for the academics, haven't I? And that means just not having the kids who can't make it in the class . . .

Notes

1 Known operationally as COSEN (Construction of Special Educational Needs), this was 'Teachers' Perspectives on Special Needs Policy and Practice', award no. R000231910. The main aim of the research was to document the experiences and effects of SEN and educational reform policies as they were expressed through LEAs and schools, and realized in the daily lives of practitioners. This aim was realized through the following objectives:

* The description and evaluation of the structures and experiences of SEN developments within four 11–16 schools in each of four LEAS.
* The exploration in depth of the experiences, attitudes and professional orientations of some 30 staff within these schools, with particular reference to the 1981 and 1988 legislation.
* The relation of teacher conceptions of SEN to policy realization.
* The development of theoretical and methodological positions within an interactionist paradigm.

The LEAs and schools which participated were identified so as to provide a range of broadly different contexts and systems. There were three overlapping phases of data collection:

* Interviews with key policy-framers in the LEAs and schools in order to build up a picture of the way in which SEN policy had developed and was constructed by those charged with developing and enacting policy.
* A questionnaire for all teachers in all participating schools, seeking information on their knowledge about and views on LEA, school and departmental policies, and about their experiences of those policies in action.
* Life-historical case studies undertaken with individual teachers to explore how their own life experiences, beliefs, attitudes and their values mediated the ways in which they interpret and develop policies.

2 Some analysis from the 1997 study is to be found in Jones (1998).

3 In 1988, the then UK government established a system whereby individual schools could 'opt out' of LEA control, receiving their funding from central government sources. Such schools took on 'grant maintained' (GM) status. Among other things, 'opting out' was decidedly favourable to schools financially (DES 1988).

References

Barton, L. (ed.) (1996) *Disability and Society: Emerging Issues and Insights* (London: Longman).

Bolton, N. (1972) *The Psychology of Thinking* (London: Cassell).

Clough, P. (1998) Bridging 'mainstream' and 'special' education: a curriculum problem. *Curriculum Studies*, 20 (4), 327–338.

Corbett, J. (1996) *'Badmouthing': The Language of Special Needs* (London: Falmer).

Corbett, J. (1998) *Special Educational Needs in the Twentieth Century: A Cultural Analysis* (London: Cassell).

Department for Education and Employment (DFEE) (1996) *Education Act 1996* (London: HMSO).

Department of Education and Science (DES) (1981) *Education Act 1981* (London: HMSO).

Department of Education and Science (DES) (1988) *Education Act 1988* (London: HMSO).

Dessent, T. (1983) *Making the Ordinary School Special* (Lewes: Falmer Press).

Golby, M. and Gulliver, R. J. (1979) Whose remedies, whose ills? A critical review of Remedial Education. *Journal of Curriculum Studies*, 11, 137–47.

Hegel, G. W. F. (1894) *Hegel's Philosophy of Mind* (trans. W. Wallace) (Oxford: Clarendon Press).

Husserl, E. (1901) *Logical Investigations*, Vols I and II (Halle: Niemeyer).

Jones, C. (1998) A study of teachers' perspectives on the inclusion of pupils with SEN in mainstream schools. Unpublished M.Sc. study, Division of Education, University of Sheffield.

Swarm, W. (1989) *Integration statistics: LEAs reveal local variations*, CSIE Factsheet (London: Centre for Studies on Integration in Education).

Wedell, K. (1985) Future directions for research on children's special educational needs. *British Journal of Special Education*, 12 (1), 22–26.

Williams, R. (1965) *The Long Revolution* (Harmondsworth: Penguin).

Source: Clough, 1999: 63–73.

Activity 3.5

Having read Clough's example of a research which was looking *for* as well as *at* and the seeking of *meanings* as well as *evidence* from which those meanings are derived, try to identify the acts of radical looking present in your own research study.

As your study progresses you will, no doubt, add to these notes in your research journal. Such changes in research strategy and construction are important developments and form part of the account of your analysis. (We shall discuss this further in Chapter 7.)

As the book develops it will become clear that *radical looking* is actually inseparable from the other radical practices which we discuss, and how radical looking – both looking *at* and looking *for* – is one of the tools of all social scientists.

CHAPTER SUMMARY

In this chapter we have:

Defined and demonstrated our view of radical looking in research and argued the importance of radical looking at all points during the research process

Outlined the function of making the familiar strange

Discussed some practices and issues of using observation as a research tool

Demonstrated, through two examples of research, different dimensions of 'radical looking': looking at; looking for; looking for evidence and looking for meanings

📖 FURTHER READING

Silverman, D. (2001) *Interpreting Qualitative Data: Methods for Analysing Talk, Text and Interaction*. London: Sage.

See particularly chapter 7 'Visual images'.

Foster, P. (1996) *Observing Schools: a Methodological Guide*. London: Paul Chapman.

Provides an overview of observational research with examples.

Listening: Issues of Voice

CHAPTER CONTENTS

LEARNING OBJECTIVES

By studying and doing the activities suggested throughout this chapter you will:

◇ have an understanding of the importance of 'voice' in social science research

◇ be aware of the literature on 'voice' in social science research

◇ have an understanding of the processes of obtaining and reporting data from focused conversation and focus groups

◇ be able to write a robust justification for generating data through group talk and writing

◇ be aware of ethical implications

◇ understand the issues and processes involved in 'interpreting' research voices.

Introduction

> *Radical listening* – as opposed
> to merely hearing – is the interpretive
> and critical means through
> which 'voice' is noticed.

In this chapter we focus specifically on the importance of 'voice' in social science research and the justifications for incorporating and interpreting research voices in particular ways. We begin with an overview of what we mean by *radical* listening: a careful attention to all the *voices* to be heard on a given topic of study. Giving prominence to 'voice' in educational and social science research emphasises our view of social research as *positional* and *political* (see Chapter 1). Having established what we mean by voice, we provide one example of developing 'method' in order to serve the research task of giving voice to a group of research participants and incorporating the researcher's voice within that experience; this example is included to illustrate the methodological structure which governs a research study. Next we further discuss issues and implications of 'giving voice' to research participants and the methodological justifications for such research. Finally, we examine some of the issues which arise when researchers attempt to 'interpret' the voices of 'others'.

'Voice' and research experience

In this section we offer an overview of what we mean by 'voice' in educational and social science research, both in terms of the voice of the researcher and the voices of the research participants.

The voices of researchers

> '... the informed researcher's voice no longer provides an
> authoritarian monologue but contributes a part to dialogue'
> (Mitchell, 1993: 55)

Research is, by definition, a search for form quite as much – and at the same time – as it is a search for 'content' or knowledge to report. As Walker (1985: 46) observes, methods are intrinsic to research, no mere adjunct but part of the unfolding story. But for the purposes of this chapter we want to take ideas of 'method' a little further, so as to get 'on the inside' of doing research. For, when Mitchell writes that

'. . . the informed researcher's voice no longer provides an authoritarian monologue but contributes a part to dialogue' 1993: 55) he is arguing that the researcher's voice is – or should be – as much present as that of the research participants.

But what does Mitchell really mean here? What might it mean for a researcher to 'contribute' to dialogue? And what form should this 'part' take? What would such research look like? Feminist research has advocated the integrity of self and research participants *in* research, and as Ann Oakley reflects on the role of 'self' in research, there is a lesson here for social science research in general:

> A feminist methodology of social science requires that this rationale of research be described and discussed not only in feminist research but in social science research in general. It requires further, that the mythology of 'hygienic' research with its accompanying mystification of the researcher and the researched as objective instruments of data production be replaced by the recognition that personal involvement is more than dangerous bias – it is the condition under which people come to know each other and to admit others into their lives. (Oakley, 1993: 58)

Activity 4.1

Consider Ann Oakley's words, and make some notes on your reflections.

What might she mean by 'the mythology of "hygienic" research'? Can you find an example of reported research which might be claimed to be 'hygienic'? Why might she consider this a 'myth'?

What might be the implications of Oakley's statement that 'personal involvement . . . is the condition under which people come to know each other and to admit others into their lives'. What are the implications of this for researchers?

The inseparability of research and researcher is, many would argue, an essential feature of research in the social sciences; and the methodology which drives such research is as much to do with personal values as it is to do with 'rigour' and 'hygiene' in research methodology. For, in a sense, methodology is as much about the way we live our lives as it is about the way in which we choose to conduct a particular piece of research. Methodology is about making research decisions and understanding (and justifying) *why* we have made those decisions. Our research methodologies are (we would argue) rooted in our own personal values which, in some form, inform our ethical and moral responses to problems and challenges. So what might we make of this in relation to the origins of our research studies? What routes (or re-routes) us to the research areas we choose?

You may well have already decided on your research questions, or at least have begun to develop the specific area in which your research will focus. Are you aware of where this interest comes from? What, for example, motivates someone to research adult literacy, or the 'deviant' behaviour of 13-year-old boys, or human rights and disability, or women's experience of higher education? What is it, in those who research, which forms that *particular* motivation?

Clough and Corbett (2000) – in tracing some routes to inclusive education – interviewed a number of influential figures in the field. Several expressed their hunches about the roots of their own research interests and their 'accidental-or-not' arrival as researchers in the field of inclusive education. Mike Oliver, for example, said:

> I think the whole issue about my own experiences as a disabled person in terms of how that has influenced my thinking as a sociological theorist and a political activist may be one of the reasons I am interested in male country and western singers. They always sing about the road and the train. They are always on a journey to somewhere. I think I've been on a journey as well, in which my own understanding of myself has changed. You know, I started out 25 years ago as a typical academic, saying 'Let's be objective. Let's study the world'. I was advised not to get into disability because it was too personal. Then I moved into recognising that personal experience gives you an added dimension to use to authenticate the work. Then I moved on to feeling that it is not an adequate model in itself either, because you are what you are. You've got to embrace rather than merely use what you are. (Oliver, 2000: 112–13)

Peter Clough picks up the theme of research/professional origins:

> I am struck by the number of people I know whose initial experience of working in special education seemed, as it were, accidental. Yet at the same time I don't really believe in this 'accidental' account; without being fatalist or therapist about it, I think that most people's involvement in 'special' education is – or becomes – knit fairly densely with their 'personal' lives and there's usually some (psycho)logic to it. (Clough, 2000: 65)

Finally, one of our own students, in respect of her own completed study of the experiences of mothers of children with disabilities, wrote:

> Selecting a topic for a dissertation according to many is a challenging task. To me, the subject I selected was an issue I was yearning to research for some time. It was about mothers' experiences of the emotional and social implications of having a child with disabilities. I wanted to tell the mothers' stories.
>
> I've always believed that parenting is a tough job and an even tougher job is parenting a child with special needs. Until I became a mother in a similar situation I had always thought that having a child with a disability always happened to someone else and possibly could never happen to you . . . It was when I found myself to be one of those mothers that I realised the daunting

task of bringing up a child with disabilities and the yawning gap between these families' experiences and the rest of the world . . . My objective was to present the personal experience of a small number of families, to tell their stories to a world which, on the whole, remains ignorant and perhaps distant from them, simply because they do not know. (Perera, 2001: 92)

Activity 4.2

We have given three examples of personal perspectives on research/careers origins. Whether or not you relate to these particular examples, we suggest that *somewhere* in your past or more present history might lie the roots of your interest.

Think about your own personal relationship to your research topic and your research questions. Write a brief paragraph or some initial notes about the derivation of your research.

It is not necessarily the case that this will prove to be an immediately revelationary exercise. We suggest that this is a point you may wish to ponder upon and, perhaps, return to the question: 'Why *are* you doing what you're doing?' And also to ask yourself: 'Do *you* think it is important to generate a response to such a question?'

Our central point here is that our *identity* – as man, woman, academic, mother, father – is (to a greater or lesser extent) a driving force in our research foci. *What* we do and *how* we do it is informed by who we are, how we think, our morals, our politics, our sexuality, our faith, our lifestyle, our childhood, our 'race', our values. In other words, we are (as researchers) our own blueprints for our research methodology. We can, in the conduct of our research, form our own specific and unique justifications for our enquiries from the existing values, morals and knowledge bases that we bring to our research. In this sense then, is it realistic to divorce ourselves from our research? Is it intellectually honest to separate our*selves*, to silence our voices as researchers within our research processes and reports? And if we choose to include our own voices in our research report, how are we to do so without risk of introspection or self-indulgence?

The voices of research participants

Clough (1998c) explores the difficulty of ' "giving" voice' in a research report of a group of 'bad lads' in a large school, fairly downtown in a poor, large city. The broad project was to understand the culture of 'special' education in that school (see Clough and Barton, 1995), but – more specifically – Clough's attempt to get a handle on the 'bad lads', draws on 'an amalgam of raw transcribed observation, interview events, notes of conversations, my own research journal and imports of my own knowing and belief' (Clough, 2002: 67) and leads him to reflect on what he calls 'inhibited voices':

> Voice does not itself struggle for rights, but is disposed after rights are established; voice is licensed by these rights. It follows from this view that the task for research is largely one of 'turning up the volume' on the depressed or inaudible voice.
>
> Listening to subjects with special educational needs throws into a particular relief all the generically difficult issues of researching 'voice' – issues to do with who is listening to whom, why and – above all, perhaps – in whose interests? For, like most research subjects in the majority of studies, they are identified because they reflect – if not quite represent – a particular population; they represent the experiences of a more or less distinct category (black males, NQTs, Y8 girls, etc); thus by definition, subjects with special educational needs are identified because they are categorically different (if not deficient). In such research they are primarily interesting, therefore, because of a perceived difference – however benignly understood, and however politically motivated the study . . .
>
> The research act of listening to voice must always involve the (broadly defined) processes of both mediation and translation; and these functions may be particularly indicated where there are doubts about the capacity of the subject to express an intention; doubts, that is, about his or her powers of articulation. This is, of course, a function of a much larger question of the power relations between the researcher and the researched.
>
> For the most part, life stories are articulated by the conventionally articulate (see Booth and Booth, 1996 for an extended discussion and bibliography). How is such advocacy justified, and at what cost? Sparkes (1994), for example, justifies such acts of writing – by people who hold advantaged positions – in terms of their more effective challenge to their privileged peers *by virtue of those positions*; he argues that studies by marginalised individuals/groups may reflect false consciousness, or may be 'coated with self-protective ideology'; and, more pragmatically, he questions whether – almost by definition – the marginalised individual possesses the resources (of various cultural capital) for effectively telling his or her own story.
>
> For some writers, the project is thus an attempt to forge dialogical empathies between the alienated, between each of our 'othernesses' (e.g., Rorty, 1989). Thus Geertz seeks to enlarge

> *the possibility of intelligible discourse between people quite different from one another in interest, outlook, wealth and power, and yet contained in a world where, tumbled as they are into endless connection, it is increasingly difficult to get out of each other's way* (1988, p.147).

But this essentially humanist (Barone,1995) project of solidarity and empathy is not enough for some story writers (and readers), who act politically through 'storied' voice specifically to emancipate; who ultimately seek, that is, a redistribution of power. Thus the search is for the articulation of a persuasive voice which will challenge readers' interests, privileges and prejudices. As bell hooks has it, such writers can provide searing, harrowing 'chronicles of pain' – though she reminds us that these may well serve merely to 'keep in place existing structures of domination' (1991, p.59) if they do not bring about a deep unease in the reader. (Clough, 2002: 68–9)

Activity 4.3

Reflect on Clough's position on 'voice' in social research. Think about the relationship between voice, power, politics and persuasion.

Is there a place in your own research for 'the articulation of a persuasive voice' which will challenge existing 'structures of domination'? Do you agree with Sparkes's stance on the writing of marginalised groups?

What are the implications of this discussion for your own work?

In the next section we shall look at one example of developing 'method' which incorporates the voices of researcher and research participants. This example demonstrates how a methodological 'frame' can underpin a research study.

Focused conversation as a research method

The following example is drawn from Nutbrown (1999). Here she discusses the origins, motivations, processes and outcomes of eliciting the 'voices' of a small group of women. As you read, bear in mind our argument that social research is persuasive, purposive, positional and political, and try to identify those features in the account.

Focused Conversation: the context

The idea of setting up a 'Focused Conversation' between a group of people grew out of my interest in understanding, eventually to write about, the practices of a particular group of under fives professionals. I wanted to know about their approach to working with parents of young children, their ideas about particular aspects of literacy, and their experiences of being black and bilingual and working in inner city areas of a large city in the north of England. I wanted to know how they worked, what informed their thinking, what they brought to their role. This account does not describe that experience per se but draws on that process to focus on the methods and methodology involved.

Writing as 'process'

The five women who were to make up the group were known to me. We had worked together on issues of practice and early education pedagogy over several years. They were the obvious group to consult when, as part of a research project focusing on ways of involving parents of young children in early literacy development, I needed advice on working bilingually with parents and their young children. It was agreed that we would work together to write about the topic.

Creating the writing process

My best exchanges with the women were our lengthy, detailed, animated conversations, so we decided to begin our work by talking. I invited them to work with me, one afternoon a week for about 10 weeks, and explained that my aim was to 'tap their expertise', learn from what they did, acknowledge the special nature of their role, write something – with them – to ensure that their part was acknowledged at every turn.

We began tentatively, despite our existing relationships which in some cases spanned more than 10 years. Here we were doing something new. We were treading new territory and we needed to proceed with care. As our first meeting began I was nervous, and very conscious of my position of power. I issued the invitation, I began the meeting, I knew what I wanted to accomplish, I had convened the group, I was seen as the academic, the authority, the writer, and I was expected to 'know'. I was conscious too of my whiteness and of my monolingualism in a group of black women all of whom were bi- (if not multi-) lingual. We had a number of things in common: we were all women, all interested in young children, and held mutual respect for our different roles in education. Those commonalities, especially the fact that we were all women, became an important dynamic in the particular working group we were to create. I am not implying that Focused Conversation research should be a 'woman only' affair – simply that it was a particularly important characteristic of this group, in this case.

There were new experiences for me, as I broke though the barriers that I perceived from my whiteness and my inability to speak any of the six other languages they spoke (Arabic, Urdu, Punjabi, Bengali, Creole, Chinese). We would work in English – our common language – but we would be talking about other languages. I anticipated that members of the group would use their other languages at times, as we worked through some details of commonalities and differences in language structure, character, heritage and etiquette. So, as we began our writing process, here was I with my one language asking people to work with me, and to do so they spoke in their second (or third) language – to help me understand more of their bilingual work.

We created a way of proceeding with our writing which, as time went on, we remoulded a little but the basic practices and processes remained the same. We worked as follows:

1 We discussed topics which had been agreed well before the writing sessions began, and added to that preliminary agenda as our work progressed and other pertinent issues emerged.

2 We negotiated how we – together – would write about the topics we discussed. One of the women said: 'It's better if we talk, Cathy, and you can write it down'. She was right of course – the richness of their experiences would only come through within fluid conversational interactions – but if I took the role as scribe for our two hour sessions I would forfeit my role as participant and be unable to make a faithful record of the conversation which was so important. I could not be a scribe in our two hour sessions and the other alternative (to include another person to act as scribe) would alter the dynamics of the group, which although newly convened for this purpose was familiar in other professional contexts. We agreed – after some reticence and inhibition – that we would tape record our sessions. We would make sure the tape 'heard' all that we said.

3 We also agreed that my role would be to take the words off the tape and apply an initial structure. The group would look at this first transcript draft and we would shape and reshape the writing from there until we were sufficiently satisfied to make our writing public.

This account draws on the experience of sessions when the group talked about being bilingual. This topic was not one which I had in mind when we began, but it emerged as a fundamental issue which we needed to explore before we could focus in any meaningful way on the topics I thought were important. So the group talked about their experiences of being young and bilingual before we moved on to our previously agreed (pre-experience) agenda.

It was at this point in creating this particular writing process that I learned I was not simply engaged in a process of gathering information in the most effective and convenient way and by a means comfortable for the 'participants' – it was here that I learned that these women were the 'data', they created new knowledge through connective discourse, as they listened and spoke together. For example on one occasion we were talking about the different home languages the women spoke:

L said, 'Arabic is a language of song and poetry. It is the most beautiful of languages'. P interjected with a gentle challenge, 'You can't just say that! You can't say your language is the most beautiful – that's because it's yours! We all think our own language is beautiful – it's because it's your own mother tongue!'

The group pursued this theme, eventually reaching agreement that it was how we felt about our own languages which was at the root of L's initial comment. Feeling about their own language was so much part of their multilingual identities.

This was the richness of this group process. One comment – one spoken thought – stimulated another and as the conversation went on a verbal sculpture was created, ideas were crafted, expressed and re-expressed as each one drew on memories of her childhood, and revisited her early life in the light of what she has just learned of another's. These were the moments when I began to think that I was engaged, not simply in a writing exercise, but a participant in a way of understanding experience which had a unique dynamism.

Our sessions had all the features of a long, animated, passionate conversation. Short pauses, long silences, discomforts, agreements, disclaimers, retractions, clarifications, humour, interruptions, repetition, emphasis, misunderstandings, excitements, conflicts, and discoveries. We created and recognised new points of convergence as we each uncovered something of our own lives and our own thinking.

Some might worry about the 'muddying' of data, of participants influencing the ideas of others, but Focused Conversation work, as I conceive it, aims to do just that – to allow for the convergence of lives and experiences. Stanley and Wise (1993 p. 161), like Oakley (1993) argue for the replacement of 'hygienic' research with the legitimisation of personal involvement:

> Our experiences suggest that 'hygienic research' is a reconstructed logic, a mythology which presents an oversimplified account of research. It is also extremely misleading, in that it emphasises the 'objective' presence of the researcher, and suggests that she can be 'there' without having any greater involvement than simple presence. In contrast, we emphasise that all research involves, as its basis, an interaction, a relationship between researcher and researched ... Because the basis of all research is a relationship, this necessarily involves the presence of the researcher *as a person*. Personhood cannot be left behind, cannot be left out of the research process.

In the case under discussion here members of the group revisited their own comments and their own assumptions in the light of what they heard from others, for example:

G made a comment about her experience in the first few weeks of infant school in England. Then she stopped and laughed and said, 'I'll have to think about what I've just said – I'm not sure I mean it!' That kind of reflection which allowed individuals to change what they said, reflect on each other's comments, and ask each other if they meant what they had said, was a rich and vital part of the writing process, one which would likely have been missed if we had chosen a different approach to this writing task.

I played a quiet role for the most part – though I did join in some debates; to put another point of view, ask for clarification, push an idea a little further. But I also noted the comments which tailed off unfinished, the thoughts that were interrupted, the threads which seemed to get lost. I noted these so that – when one theme seemed to be finished or exhausted – I could return to that thought. I would say things like: 'C – you were talking about your first teacher' or 'G – a moment ago you mentioned a time in Jamaica when ...' I did this to try to capture every gem of experience that they were sharing.

I also noted those who did not speak for some time, but was careful not to try to draw them into the conversation too soon because they might well have been participating whilst silent, engaged in listening and reflecting on what they heard. As Lewis (1992) notes with regard to group interviewing, people can take thinking time. The dynamics of this group were such that on occasions people sank back in their chairs, perhaps reflecting on what they heard, trying out some idea in their head. People concentrated to different degrees and levels of intensity at different times throughout our two-hour sessions; boiled the kettle again, left the room for five minutes, without pressure and in the knowledge that silent thought and times of apparent non-contribution were legitimised, even recognised as necessary factors in what was at times a quite intense process.

The writing as 'product'

We were conscious that we were writing to produce a product which would eventually be made public. The writing went through nine drafts and each time new words were added, new thoughts created, old thoughts discarded – or withdrawn from the public eye. What was created was a short piece of writing which told much about the women's experiences and which humbled me as the privileged 'participant' who was allowed to listen to and help compose their stories. In a sense, the product of the process – the finished, public writing – is not so important, what is more important is the process by which data can be created, moulded and reported as a seamless process. What is different about this writing which emerges from focused conversation work is that the group participants do not simply provide the quotes, they co-author the whole piece.

Seeking the method that 'feels' right

'Selection of methods may be an act of faith rather than a rational response to a clearly formulated problem. The method may even be an intrinsic part of the problem, rather than extrinsic and disconnected from it. Just as recipes are not simply things that are done to food, but become concepts within which method and substance are compounded, so 'method' in research can become an intrinsic part of the project. *The methods we choose are, in this sense, there to be tested, just as much as the substantive hypothesis.*'

(Walker, 1985, p.46 our italics)

There were other alternatives to the process of Focused Conversation which I have described. Instead of opting for a process of collaborative writing I could have chosen to obtain information from the five individuals concerned, weave this information together in the way I saw fit, consult them on a draft and eventually publish with appropriate acknowledgement to them for their contribution. The most obvious alternative to this collaborative writing process was first to use individual interviews with each person.

Considering interviews

I could have set about interviewing each of the five women – having some idea before hand of what we might talk about. This would either have necessitated considerable time and several one-to-one interviews with each person first to establish the agenda and then to explore them with each individual or, as Seidman puts it, to share and understand something of 'other people's stories' (Seidman, 1991, p.1).

> Telling stories is essentially a meaning-making process. When people tell stories, they select details from their stream of consciousness ... It is this process of selecting constitutive details of experience, reflecting on them, giving them order, and thereby making sense of them that makes telling stories a meaning-making experience.
>
> (Seidman, 1991, p.1)

What I was interested in was not simply their stories and experiences of work with young children but also the way in which their collective experiences fitted together.

Individual 'long interviews' as discussed by McCracken (1988) might well have provided rich data which could then be analysed according to the categories which I identified as meaningful when I came to analyse the transcripts. Such an approach would have yielded five separate sets of interview scripts – of varying depth – for me to analyse as I saw fit, and it would have been my responsibility to mould their five unique and individual experiences and ideas into a structure that I created. The main disadvantage of this method – for me – lay in the 'separateness' of the five responses, when part of the objective was to understand something of the 'collective' experiences of the group. The aim of this process was not as McCracken puts it to 'survey the terrain' but to 'mine it' (p.17). The method for this piece of exploration needed to suit a process which was 'much more intensive than extensive in its objectives' (McCracken, 1988, p.17).

The right 'feeling' is seldom discussed as a rationale for deciding on methods of data collection and analysis in educational research but here, for me, it figured highly, and I suggest that 'feeling' (or perhaps we might say 'hunch') is an important methodological consideration. Neither interviews, questionnaires or individual writing 'felt' right for the task. Somehow – for this particular group of women and this particular task – the accepted research methods of obtaining information did not fit. At the time my aim was to obtain information in order to write some material about a specific topic – I was not (I thought) engaged so much in research as in a process of writing a practical booklet for early childhood educators. I needed a means of gathering the information which would eventually lead to a publishable written outcome. I was seeking some way of combining the richness of detail and experience which could be obtained from long interviews with shared consensus and collective meaning-making which involved all participants. Lewis (1992) discussed the usefulness of group interviews with children suggesting that this was a useful tool for achieving consensus and evolving views where there could be some element of 'connecting with' or, as Lewis terms it, 'tagging on' (p.416) to the ideas of other interview participants.

Some thoughts on Procedures and Processes in Focused Conversations

So how might this experience of a writing process help to shape a research method? Key elements in this particular writing project can be extracted and developed as some kind of guideline on procedures and processes for the use of 'Focused Conversations' in educational research. In doing this I do not want to add methodological complication or construct some pretence of 'rigour' – often processes of writing (and research methods) can be constrained under the guise of rigour or 'quality control'. There are perhaps some characteristics of the specific writing process described above which contributed to its success and which might be used to develop a frame within which other Focused Conversation research can be conducted. The following characteristics are not intended as a blue print – merely as a 'recipe' (to use Walker's metaphor) to be tried and tasted. It may well be that for some new ingredients must be added and others removed – it depends on the research questions, the circumstances and the participants. It depends on what kind of meal you want to cook, and who will eat of it!

What might make Focused Conversations a useful research tool?

- Familiarity of members of the group
- A group large enough to be a group but small enough for everyone to have a voice (say 4 – 7)
- An agreed topic of shared experience, knowledge and interest
- Willingness to explore statements and ideas in terms of individuals' own experiences and personal histories
- Willingness and desire to – eventually – make this exploration or the outcomes of it public
- The expectations of the 'researcher' – responsibilities, ethical considerations
- The role of the 'researcher' as group convenor and 'caretaker' of proceedings
- Mutual respect for opinions, culture, experience – everyone has something to offer
- Established confidentiality

There are established methods in educational and social science research which might be viewed as similar to the Focused Conversation. It is important to locate work using focused conversations within the context of other established methods – if only to avoid some accusation of mis-use of other methods!

Focus Group Interviews

I would not want what I am suggesting here to be misconstrued as a misinterpretation (or poor use!) of the Focus Group interview. My understanding is that this is a somewhat different process.

Though some definitions suggest similarities between Focus Group Interviews and Focused Conversations, processes are different.

First some definitions of focus group interviews:

'an informal discussion among selected individuals about specific topics relevant to the situation at hand'

(Beck, Trombetta, and Share, 1986, p. 73)

'organised group discussions which are focused around a single theme'

(Byers and Wilcox, 1988, p. 1)

'The goal of focus group interviews is to create a candid, normal conversation that addresses, in depth, the selected topic'.

(Vaughn, Schumm & Sunagub, 1996, p. 4)

In describing the processes of Focus Group Interviews, Hess (1968) notes the advantages of this technique over individual interviews to include:

1 **synergism** (when a wider bank of data emerges through the group interaction)
2 **snowballing** (when the statements of one respondent initiate a chain reaction of additional comments)
3 **stimulation** (when the group discussion generates excitement about a topic)
4 **security** (when the group provides a comfort and encourages candid responses)
5 **spontaneity** (when participants are not required to answer every question, their responses are more spontaneous and genuine).

(Hess, 1968)

Vaughn, Schumm, & Sunagub (1996) set out five reasons for using focus group interviews:

1 Focus Group Interviews offer variety and versatility to both qualitative and quantitative research methods
2 Focus Group Interviews are compatible with the qualitative research paradigm
3 Focus Group Interviews offer opportunities for direct contact with subjects
4 The Group Format offers distinctive advantages for data collection (encourages interaction; encourages openness; allows and encourages formation of opinions through interaction with others)
5 Focus group interviews offer utility.

So far, so good, but these authors then go on to set out an 8 step plan describing how the FGI should be conducted. With rigid rules for a 'moderator' and stringent guidelines on data analysis. A key difference between Focus Group interviews and Focused Conversation research is that, with the former, the role of participants often ends with the completion of data collection. For me Focused Conversations can continue to involve participants in the development of data to analysis and reporting.

Others have defended focus group interviews against critics:

'Focus Group research has been the subject of much controversy and criticism. Such criticism is generally associated with the view that focus groups interviews do not yield 'hard' data, and the concern that group members may not be representative of a larger population (because of both the small numbers and the idiosyncratic nature of the group discussion). Such criticism, however, is unfair. Although focus groups do have important limitations of which the researcher should be aware, limitations are not unique to focus group research; all research tools in the social sciences have significant limitations.'

(Stewart and Shamdasani, 1990, p.12)

It is interesting that the strengths are not identified as lying in their idiosyncratic nature. The group is not necessarily a representative 'sample' nor is what they say immediately generalisable, they simply provide a collective viewpoint of those present (at that time) in that composition. It is a story, a single account (that is what it is and it need not claim to be anything else). If generalisable findings or representative samples are needed then, arguably, different methods should be used.

Stewart and Shamdasani (1990) identify many potential problems and issues in terms of the group being composed/assembled particularly for the purpose of the research. In the work I have described here the group already existed. Issues of importance that emerged within this group lead to the development of the method of working which I am calling Focused Conversation, in order to stimulate the writing process. Issues of data analysis, also discussed in depth by Stewart and Shamdasani (1990), are rendered less important when the group are the data, the analysts and the authors.

The Focus Group Interview in social science research originating in consumer and market research is a very different method from the focus group work described by Madriz (1998) who, researching the lives of women describes her use of focus groups as:

> The singularity of the focus group as a form of collective testimony is that it allows women to exchange, verify, and confirm their experiences with other women of similar socioeconomic and ethnic backgrounds (Jarrett 1993). The interaction in focus groups emphasises empathy and commonality of experiences and fosters self-disclosure and self-validation. Communication among women can be an awakening experience and an important element of a consciousness-raising process because it asserts women's rights to substantiate their own experiences.
>
> (Madriz, 1998, p. 116)

Madriz (1998) describes her use of focus groups to elicit life stories and experiences, her description of the groups, located in a feminist research perspective, is different from those focus groups convened and written about by some male researchers who set out with some precision details of the Focus Group method itself. Perhaps this attention to detail of procedure is in part to prevent the 'method' itself being distorted (Morgan, 1998). In contrast, feminist paradigms continue to seek new research ways which, more honestly, include the researcher. (This is not to say that such tools are only used by women researchers – but it does appear that feminist paradigms push at the boundaries of method.) Fine (1994) writes of her need to place herself in her research:

> The interviews with the Baltimore women forced us to come clean; I had to reinsert consciously my interpretive self into my writings, with, but not through, the rendition of their voices. Researchers cannot write about/with/through adults' (or adolescents') voices as if the researchers had 'said it all'.
>
> (Fine, 1994, p. 22)

The Focused Conversation which I am exploring as a method is more closely aligned, one could say 'rooted', in the Individual Focused Interview as used in Oral/Life History research than in those methodologically controlled Focus Group Interviews. But Focused Conversation work goes further than Focus Group Interviews which stop at the generation of data. Focused Conversation work in my interpretation is not complete until participants have agreed their written version of the events. For Madriz, as with most researchers, most of the time, the power of authorship rested with her:

> I see my role as being part of the broader group of researchers who translate women's experiences ... to the reader with the intent of advancing social justice and social change and writing against 'othering'. I am aware, however, that my particular translation of these women's voices is possible because of my middle-class background and particularly because of my education, which gives power to my translation, making it 'scholarly' work.
>
> (Madriz, 1998, p. 117)

The creation of new knowledge – Focused Conversations in Educational and Social Science Research

So, what, if anything, does this 'method' offer to the function of research? How does research using Focused Conversations help to create new knowledge? What place might the Focused Conversation have in Research in Educational and Social Science Research? Through 'talking-for-writing' new ideas can be born, new knowledge can be created, views can be shaped and re-shaped. The richness of the process lies in the openness of those who participate and their willingness to allow their ideas to be shaped by those of others, and to examine their own experiences in the light of what they hear others say. It is a process of thinking, where the thoughts – every spoken thought – is captured on tape for future reflection.

Later examination of the first draft of the transcribed tape can lead to a new composition. People may say things like:'I didn't say that ... well maybe I said it but I don't mean it like that – I mean ... ' And that thought, that idea is reshaped again.

The processes I have described here form, for me, one of those new paths in the relationship between 'researcher' and 'research participants'.

For me the value of Focused Conversations in educational and social science research lies in the process of holding on to the talk, reshaping talk and creating a dynamic where one person allows another's words to illuminate and sometimes rephrase their own. Inestimable is the process by which the sources of the data become analysts of those data and eventually become the authors of what is written from those processes, and the blurring of boundaries between researcher and researched. The words we speak are not always the ones we want but our own words reflected back a week later off the page, can trigger new ideas as well as clarify existing ones (and again, and again) until our written words say what we are content to say to others whom we may never know.

This process may well transfer to situations where it is people's thoughts, feelings and experiences which we want to capture (indeed our own when we become part of the process). It is a method of gathering data out of our heads, a research method which, like other forms of data gathered, eventually leads to writing. Focused Conversations are about voices, experiences, stories and their place in research; about finding new words, new expressions and new learning about ourselves in a shared dynamic of communication. What is different in this process is that those who are the data, are those who gather the data, remould and reshape the data, analyse those data, draft and redraft the words which result until the paper is written (and has – in the process – become research).

Source: Nutbrown, 1999: 4–22

Activity 4.4

Before you move on, reflect on the example above. Make some notes on the usefulness of generating, interpreting and reporting data through focused conversations in the context of your own research study.

Would a method like this be useful in your own study? Is its methodological frame one which would support the structures which drive your own research?

'Interpretation' of research voices

There is always an ethical problem surrounding issues of 'interpretation'. Just how does a researcher make sense of data derived from the voices of others? Numerous texts on research methods set out 'the method' and include details of 'how to' analyse data. However, it is still a matter (always) of interpretation. Researchers adopt a variety of practices in order to make meaning from the information given to them and garnered in different ways. Hannon and Nutbrown (2001) reported a large longitudinal randomised control design experimental study. It involved much statistical data but also included the voices of over 500 participants: parents, children and teachers. The research report 'gives voice' to the research participants before it presents the outcomes of quantitative data. The interpretation of research voices is not an issue to be confined to purely qualitative or ethnographic research. The important point here is 'faithful' interpretation of what is heard, arising from *radical listening* which has the characteristics of honesty and integrity.

It is generally the case in research studies that interpretation is the job of the researcher. But is there a case in particular studies – on particular topics – for placing interpretation in the hands of the participants? Perhaps, this is what Fine might call 'playing with power' (Fine, 1994: 23). 'Playing' it may be, but is this a means by which we can trust that the story told is the story as the participants want to tell it? This means more than returning to the 'participants' or 'interviewees' with a transcript; it means more than asking them to 'approve' a final draft. It means involving them in writing the story – drafting and redrafting, worrying over words and interpretations, thinking about 'the reader' until they (until we) are happy to make our writing public. The power and responsibility of authorship is held in collective.

Tierney (1998) and others who work through narrative and life history research (Clough, 1996; Kiesinger, 1998) consider the place of the researched self and 'others' in the process of research and in the text created. Tierney concludes: 'To seek new epistemological and methodological avenues demands that we chart new paths rather than constantly return to well-worn roads and point out that they will not take us where we want to go' (Tierney, 1998: 68).

Reflecting on his own work Clough considers the work which results from his own project to explore aspects of 'self' in his research:

> In 1996 I published a story called *Again, Fathers and Sons* [Clough, 1996], a story 'about' Klaus, a 9-year-old boy with moderate learning difficulties, and emotional and behavioural difficulties which had already seen him excluded from two schools. I met him when I worked in the residential unit where he had been placed. Of the 'facts', I should record that this boy and his father 'existed' as they do in the story; my visit to the house and the father's visit to the school 'happened' in precisely the way that my memory reconstructs them in the story. In this sense, there is no *material* import to the story. But its data have no formal record, and its particular structure is achieved through a working out of a very personal agenda and it is verified only in collision with the experience of the reader.
>
> Any discussion of the story of '*Klaus*' insists upon particular consideration of research and self. The role of the researcher's self in the construction of research accounts is a ground being cleared in the increasing occupation of educational research with the insertion of the researcher her/himself in the process of research. Reflections on research collected, for example, by Walford (1991), Vulliamy & Webb (1992), and Clough & Barton (1995) emphasise the growing critical, but also reflexive self-awareness of educational enquiry, and in the introductions to each of these collections is seen the impulse to such revelation located and justified in a particular tradition of human science study.
>
> Klaus and I are central to the story – but it is my own identity which lies at the heart of the meaning constructed through this story – a kind of 'testament' (Hutton-Jarvis 1999). My own identity as I constructed it in relation to my own father is central too – stripped as I was of power and confidence in the presence of this other father. (Clough, 2002: 107)

Confidentiality or secrecy?

All research must be interrogated for the means by which it 'protects' the interests of the participants. Researchers make their own decisions about how their subjects' 'confidences' are protected in the reporting of research. Clough admitted some of his struggles with his own father as he searched his 'fossils' in order to understand himself *in* his research. But aside from the standard (and essential) ethical undertakings of confidentiality there may be issues of secrecy to think about. Mitchell, in his book *Secrecy in Fieldwork* (1993), points out that the researcher's relationships with those he/she studies are of the heart and of the mind: they are, he says, 'inseparably and simultaneously both cognitive and affective . . .' (Mitchell, 1993: 12). He goes on:

> Looking inward, researchers face the greatest dangers, the dangers of self-doubt and questioned identity. Secrecy, always present, is also always double-edged . . .
>
> At risk is the potential of researchers to equivocate in this challenge and rest their ethical cases on methodological routines, while as social selves they remain outsiders, objective analysts with their one over reaching agendas. Researchers may fail fundamentally to meet the most crucial of fiduciary responsibilities, the responsibility for informed reporting of members' perspectives . . .
>
> In insisting on expressive distance, in conducting work from positions of convenience, in relative power of control, researchers may achieve only incomplete understandings . . .
>
> In order to understand, researchers must be more than technically competent. They must enter into cathected intimacies, open themselves to their subjects' feeling worlds, whether those worlds are congenial to them or repulsive. They must confront the duality of represented and experienced selves simultaneously, both conflicted, both real . . .
>
> Finally and fundamentally, the fieldworkers understand. They can keep no secrets from themselves. In action of consequence, there is no frontier between appearing and being. (Mitchell, 1993: 54–5)

All researchers are on the 'inside' of their research. Some open themselves up to the secrets which insider perspectives reveal and some admit the secrets.

Activity 4.5

Issues of self, voice and secrecy have a direct relation to that of interpretation of research voices in any research study, whatever the scale.

Think of the people who may participate – in different ways – in your research. Whose voices might you want to listen to?

What are the implications of *radical listening* and 'giving voice' to research participants for: your research design; research questions; data collection; interpretation; and report?

Issues of 'voice', 'self' and 'interpretation' are themes which are also addressed in later chapters. In Part III we shall see how radical listening – as opposed to merely hearing – is central to the development of a good research design and writing a compelling report.

CHAPTER SUMMARY

In this chapter we have:

Discussed issues of 'voice' and research experience

Provided an example of raising, interpreting and reporting voices through focused conversation, and discussed the use of focused conversation as a research method

Explored the methodological issues which arise in the attempt to 'give voice' to research participants

Discussed the 'interpretation' of research 'voices'

📖 FURTHER READING

The following readings provide additional information on Focus Group methods:

Vaughn, S., Shay, J., Schumm, J. and Sinagub, J. (1996) 'Focus group interviews – introduction', in S. Vaughn, J. Shay, J. Schumm and J. Sinagub, *Focus Group Interviews in Education and Psychology*. London: Sage, pp. 1–10.

For work on 'voice' and interpretation of research voices see:

Clough, P. and Barton, B. (eds) (1998) *Articulating with Difficulty: Research Voices in Inclusive Education*. London: Paul Chapman.

Anderson, K., Armitage, S., Jack, D., and Wittner, J. (1990) 'Beginnning where we are: feminist methodology in oral history', in J. McCarl Nielsen (ed.), *Feminist Research Methods: Exemplary Readings in the Social Sciences*. London: Westview Press.

Reading: Purpose and Positionality

CHAPTER CONTENTS

LEARNING OBJECTIVES

By studying and doing the activities in this chapter you will:

◇ have an understanding of *radical reading*

◇ develop an awareness of the place of criticality in radical reading of both texts and practices

◇ have explored examples of critical responses to literature

◇ have responded to examples of critical readings of events

◇ have developed your own definition and synopsis of the place of criticality in your own research

Introduction

> *Radical reading* provides the justification for the critical adoption
> or rejection of existing knowledge and practices.

In this chapter we discuss the centrality of the literature search and review and the 'readings' of the research settings in which researchers work.

Building on our argument that social research is *purposive* and *positional*, we argued in Chapter 2 that *radical reading* is a process which exposes the *purposes* and *positions* of both texts and practices. By using the word 'reading' here we are concerned both with the understanding of written texts and the more metaphorical 'reading' of situations – 'How do *you* read this or that action or event?' How, that is, do you interpret the events in the theatre of enquiry?

Activity 5.1

Take a moment to reflect on our definition of *radical reading*. How does this concept help you in your research study? Make some brief notes in your research journal. Remember that is it important not necessarily to agree with our position, but rather to engage with it.

Criticality

> *Criticality* – 'being critical' – describes the attempt to show *on
> what terms* 'personal' and 'public' knowledges are jointly
> articulated – and therefore where their *positional* differences lie.

Any critical account seeks to be *rational*, but will also reflect the values and beliefs of its author. It is the presence of the *persuasive* in a critical account which reveals the full range of values at work.

In Chapter 1 we asked, *What is research?* and outlined the specific characteristics of social research as *persuasive, purposive, positional* and *political*. Alongside these important *characteristics* of social research it is necessary to establish an operational understanding of the phases involved in any research study. Such an understanding of the *constructural features* of social research becomes central at this point in our discussion. In a simple operational definition we could say that social research consists of six steps.

We want to demonstrate here how *radical reading* is inseparable from the other three radical processes discussed elsewhere in this book, and show how it is essential in realising the six steps presented in Figure 5.1. In the following scheme (Figure 5.2) we connect these six steps with the various *radical processes* in the conduct of *critical enquiry.*

Operationally, research consists of:

1 *framing* a research question;

2 *finding out* what existing answers there are to that question;

3 *establishing* what is 'missing' from those answers, then,

4 *getting information* which will answer the question; and,

5 *making meanings* from the information which helps to answer your research question,

6 *presenting a report* which highlights the significance of your study.

Figure 5.1   *Six steps in critical social science enquiry*

Activity 5.2

Think about the simple six-step operational structure above. Can it be applied to your own study? In which ways can the various radical acts of critical social science enquiry be identified as present in your own study?

The critical literature review

In this section we shall examine what *radical reading* means in relation to the literature. First we shall describe practical strategies for *radical reading* of research reports. Second we suggest how research questions will inform the literature search decisions. Finally we shall look at some examples of demonstrating a critical response to such reading in the writing of research reports.

Practically *radical reading means asking the following questions of what you read:*

- *What is the author trying to say?*
  What is the real point here? What is the central argument?
- *To whom is the author speaking?*
  Is this account written for academics? Policy-makers? Practitioners? Is the author really speaking to me?
- *Why has this account of this research been written?*
  Does s/he have a political point to make? How does this relate to current policy?

Operational step	Radical processes
1 *Framing* a research question	This cannot be successfully achieved without some *radical reading* of the research literature and/or the 'theatre' of research
2 *Finding out* what existing answers there are to that question	Essential here is engagement with the research literature – *critical reading*
3 *Establishing* what is 'missing' from those answers	Some *radical looking* is necessary here – seeing beyond the known – to find the precise focus of the study which makes your study unique. Criticality in the *radical reading* of literature and 'theatre'
4 *Getting information* which will answer the question	More reading of the literature and *radical listening* and *looking* in the generation of data
5 *Making meanings* from the information which helps to answer your research question	*Radical looking* and *radical reading* of the meanings within the evidence at the stage of analytical interpretation of data; *critical reflection*
6 *Presenting a report* which highlights the significance of your study	Telling the research story. Accounting for the findings through the research report in *persuasive* ways which make explicit the findings, the *purpose* or the study, the *position* of the researcher and the *political* nature of the research act. The research report brings together these *radical processes* of *Looking, Listening, Questioning* and *Reading* and ultimately *justifies* the enquiry

Figure 5.2 *Six operational steps and their radical processes of critical social science enquiry*

- *What does the author ultimately want to achieve?*
  Does s/he want to bring about some change? Does s/he want to make a difference? To what?
- *What authority does s/he appeal to?*
  Disciplinarity? Policy evidence? Political mission?
- *What evidence does the author offer to substantiate the claims?*
  Participants' statements? Observations/documentary analysis? Is there any 'missing' evidence?
- *Do I accept this evidence?*
  Is it sufficient to support the claims made in the report? What else could I ask to see?

- *Does this account accord with what I know of the world?*
  Is there a match between my experience and my reading and what I am reading? Does it matter if the report is disconnected from my own world? Can I learn something from that disconnection?
- *What is my view?*
  Based on what principles/ideology/pedagogy/life experiences . . . and supported by which authors . . . ?
- *What evidence do I have for this view?*
  How can I substantiate my own view? Do I draw on what I am reading here? What other sources and experiences have formed my view?
- *Do I find this account credible within the compass of my experience and knowledge?*
  Taking my responses to the above questions, does my reading of this research report lead me to decide that it should 'count' in my own study? Should it be included as part of the bank of information and evidence which shapes my own study?

It is perhaps helpful to think of radical reading as posing two sets of questions: questions to the author and questions put, as it were, 'to myself'. The questions in Figure 5.3 can be used when reading any piece of research literature and offer a distinct and straightforward strategy for making a critical response to what you are reading.

Questions to 'ask' the author . . .	Questions to ask myself . . .
Why did you write this?	Why am I reading this?
Who did you write this for?	Was it written for 'me'?
What was your purpose?	What am I looking for?
What questions were you asking?	What questions am I asking?
What answers did you find?	Do I find those answers credible?
What is your evidence?	Do I accept that evidence?
What is your conclusion?	Do I agree with those conclusions?
	But above all . . . *What have I learned?* *and* *How can I use it?*

Figure 5.3   Critical reading: some questions

Activity 5.3

With the questions in Figure 5.3 in mind, try reflecting on something you've read recently – a magazine or newspaper article perhaps.

To what extent do you use the strategies for critical reading suggested above to decide on the usefulness of the piece *for your purposes?*

The 'Crowsfoot' questions

In Chapter 2 we showed how our students arrived at two research questions which would help them to respond to issues raised by the headteacher at Crowsfoot School. The questions were:

1 To what extent do the attitudes of staff affect the inclusion of children with learning difficulties in Crowsfoot School?
2 What steps might be taken to develop more inclusive attitudes and practices at Crowsfoot?

These questions are pivotal in planning a suitably focused *literature search* and in writing a critical *literature review*. One technique for planning a literature search from research questions is to map the key themes on to a Venn diagram. It can help to try to identify three key themes from the research questions in order to develop sufficient focus for the search. The most likely key themes for the Crowsfoot study literature search are: teacher attitudes, inclusive education and learning difficulties. If these are mapped on to the Venn diagram as in Figure 5.4, the precise focus of the literature search becomes clear. This is the literature which lies in the intersection of the three key themes (marked 'Literature search' in Figure 5.4).

This means of focusing in, from the research questions, to the key themes in the literature and finding what lies at the heart of the study provides a simple but effective tool for identifying the key terms for a literature search and for making decisions about what to include and what to leave outside the scope of the study.

Literature and positionality

Finally, in this section, we want to consider the role of the literature in demonstrating positionality. Typically, all research reports (especially those written for award bearing courses) include some form of literature review. One function of the *critical literature review* is to locate the *positionality* of the research being reported within its field and to identify how that research is *unique*.

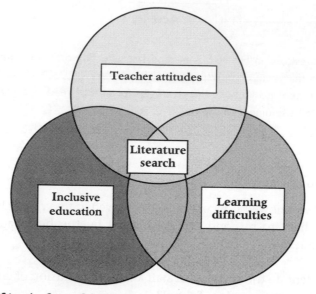

Figure 5.4   *Identifying the focus of the literature search*

The following extract from a research journal shows how Hannon and Nutbrown (1997) summarised the literature in their field of study and identified what was *unique* in their own research report. We have included the 'Abstract' so as to give an overview of the whole article and then the 'Introduction' which uses the literature to position the research and its researchers and, in the final sentence, to state the uniqueness of the study being reported.

Teachers' use of a Conceptual Framework for Early Literacy Education involving Parents

PETER HANNON & CATHY NUTBROWN
University of Sheffield, United Kingdom

ABSTRACT Changes in literacy education regarding the importance of early years and the role of parents have implications for teacher professional development which have not yet been fully addressed. This article describes a conceptual frame-work intended to give early childhood educators a way of thinking about the role of parents in children's early literacy development and how teachers can work with parents. The conceptual framework was offered to a group of teachers through a professional development programme of six seminars. Four sources of data were used to evaluate the meaningfulness of the framework, its perceived usefulness to teachers, and its impact on practice. Findings indicate that the framework largely achieved its intended purposes but some issues requiring further development and investigation are identified.

Introduction

Two aspects of literacy education have changed radically in recent years: first, recognition of the importance of the early stages of children's literacy development, particularly in the pre-school years; and second, acknowledgement of the value of parental involvement, again in particular in the early years. Both have implications for the professional development of early years teachers. In this article we argue that the need is to offer teachers concepts for understanding early literacy development, the parents' role in that development and the teacher's role in relation to the parents. We propose a particular conceptual framework to aid understanding of these issues and report an evaluation of it which involved investigating teachers' views of the framework and studying how it enabled them to develop new practice in early literacy education.

Recognition of the importance of the early stages of children's literacy development has come about as a result of several lines of research. Simple measures of literacy development at school entry (e.g. ability to recognise or form letters, book handling skills) have been shown to be powerful predicators of later attainment – better, arguably, than other measures of ability or oral language development (Wells, 1987; Tizard et al., 1988). Other predictors from as early as 3 years of age include knowledge of nursery rhymes (Maclean et al., 1987) and having favourite books (Weinberger, 1996). The teaching implications of these findings are not straightforward (for it does not follow that concentrating directly on any of these things will, in itself improve later literacy attainment) but it is at least clear that early literacy experiences of some kind are important. Research has also given us a fuller appreciation of the nature of literacy development in the pre-school period – what Yetta Goodman has termed the 'roots of literacy' which, she argues, often go unnoticed (Goodman, 1980, 1986). Particularly interesting is what children learn from environmental print – a major feature of the print-rich cultures of the Western world – which for some children may be more influential than books. Children's early writing development can also be traced back into the pre-school period, especially if one looks at children's understanding of the function of writing as well as its form (Teale and Sulzby, 1986; Hall, 1987). Other aspects of early literacy development to have been highlighted by researchers include phonological awareness (Goswami and Bryant, 1990), understanding of narrative and story (Meek, 1982; Wells, 1987), and decontextualised talk (Snow, 1991).

Acknowledgement of the value of parental involvement in the teaching of literacy at all ages has also been the result of a large number of research studies (Dickinson, 1994; Hannon, 1995; Wolfendale and Topping, 1996). In the early years, children do not acquire their knowledge of written language unaided – parents and other family members have a central role. A survey by Hannon and James (1990) found parents of pre-school children, across a wide range of families, to be very active in promoting children's literacy. Most would have appreciated support from nursery teachers but did not get it. Some parents go so far as deliberately to teach their children some aspects of literacy (Farquhar et al., 1985; Hall at al., 1989; Hannon and James, 1990). However, although virtually all parents attempt to assist pre-school literacy in some way, they do not all do it in the same way, to the same extent, with the same concept of literacy, or with the same resources (Heath, 1983; Taylor, 1983; Wells, 1987; Taylor and Dorsey-Gaines, 1988; Hannon et al., 1991). Much of the variation in children's early literacy achievement must be due to what parents do, or do not do, at home in the pre-school years.

There is ample encouragement therefore to involve parents in early literacy education, but how that can best be achieved and the implications for teachers' professional development have not been adequately explored (Nutbrown et al., 1991). Part of the problem is that teachers are trained for their role in promoting children's classroom literacy learning. Children's home literacy learning may well be more important but, by its nature, it is usually invisible to schoolteachers, who are not necessarily well equipped conceptually to appreciate its nature or power.

Teachers' concepts of literacy learning have been the subject of several research studies. For example, in adult literacy education there has been research into how teachers' implicit theories structure their classroom practice (Dirkx and Spurgin, 1992). In the school years, studies have also concentrated on teachers' conceptions of classroom instruction and learning (Martin, 1982; DeFord, 1985; Levande, 1989; Wham, 1993; Guimares and Youngman, 1995). Some authors have noted the significance of children's out-of-school or pre-school learning and explored the implications for how teachers conceptualise what they offer in classrooms (Duffy and Anderson, 1984; Weir, 1989; Cambourne, 1995; Barclay et al., 1995; Anderson, 1995), but there appears to have been little concern for how teachers might influence that literacy learning through work with parents. In this article we want to consider how a particular conceptual framework might provide the means for teachers to do just that.

Source: Hannon and Nutbrown, 1997: 405–20.

Note how, having reviewed the literature and positioned their own study within that literature, the authors state in the last two sentences what it is precisely that makes this study unique – what contribution to knowledge this *particular* research study in this *particular* research report is making. The article goes on to explain aspects of early literacy development and the four roles which the authors suggest parents can play in their children's early literacy development: providing *opportunities, recognition, interaction* and a *model* of a literacy user (Hannon and Nutbrown, 1997: 407). They suggest that the various strands of literacy (as identified through the literature review) and the four parents' roles can be combined in a heuristic device which they call the ORIM (*opportunities, recognition, interaction* and a *model*) framework (Figure 5.5).

STRANDS OF EARLY LITERACY DEVELOPMENT

		Environmental print	Books	Writing	Oral language
FAMILIES	*Opportunities*				
CAN	*Recognition*				
PROVIDE	*Interaction*				
	Model				

Figure 5.5   *The ORIM framework*
Source: Hannon and Nutbrown, 1997.

Having used the literature to establish a theoretical basis for this framework (in Figure 5.5) Hannon and Nutbrown (1997) go on to locate the literature they have reviewed in terms of their framework. They map onto the framework, the studies they have reviewed (Figure 5.6), thus using the framework to critically review the

STRANDS OF EARLY LITERACY DEVELOPMENT

		Environmental print	Books	Writing	Oral language
FAMILIES	*Opportunities*	J	B C D E G H I J K L M N	E F J	A N?
CAN	*Recognition*	J	E G H I J M N?	E J	N?
PROVIDE	*Interaction*	J	B E G H I? J M N	E F J	A N?
	Model	J	E? H J	E? F J	A

Figure 5.6   *The ORIM framework: analysis of previous research studies*
Source: Hannon and Nutbrown 1997: 409.

Key:
A = Wade (1984); B = Swinson (1985); C = McCormick and Mason (1986); D = Griffiths and Edmonds (1986); E = Lujan et al. (1986); F = Green (1987); G = Edwards (1989); H = Goldsmith and Handel (1990); I = Winter and Rouse (1990); J = Hannon et al. (1991); K = Segel and Freidberg (1991); L = Wade and Moore (1993); M = Arnold and Whitehurst (1994); N = Toomey and Sloane (1994).

literature they cite in terms of the home-focused early literacy education. This action provides *evidence* – as a result of *critical reading* and a form of *radical looking* – that most work in the field in which Hannon and Nutbrown were working was more narrowly focused than their own and that some cells in the framework had been largely neglected by researchers. Thus the territory in which Hannon and Nutbrown located their own research was established without ambiguity.

Using a similar device for critical reflection, Nutbrown (1997) reviewed a number of measures of literacy in terms of her stated desirable characteristics. Having provided an extensive overview of existing measures she summarised them in tabular form (Figure 5.7) to identify the contribution those particular studies make to the field and – importantly – to demonstrate what was unique about Nutbrown's (1997) own study.

Critical interpretations of events

So far we have discussed the role of *radical reading* in terms of developing a critical response to literature. Otherwise, and in the actual field, many aspects of research involve 'reading' the research setting as well as reading the literature in the substantive and related fields of enquiry. But what does it mean to take a 'reading' of a research situation? At its simplest level, it involves the researcher in reading – literally – from noticeboards, institution policy documentation, corridors of public buildings and other signs and signals – as well as more subtle data such as body language in interviews or meetings or other interactive settings. The interpretation of silences and well as spoken responses also form part of taking a 'reading' of the setting. Such (in-part) 'intuitive' data is often disregarded but can play a powerful role in forming the researchers' response to work with/in the research setting. Experiences which require an interpretational 'reading' in order to understand the actions and interactions within the situation must also be considered in the forming of research questions and the making of research decisions.

What follows are two examples of writing which emanate from the researcher's 'intuitive' reading of research settings. They are based on data gathered through *radical reading* of each research setting: grafitti, local newspaper reports, postures of staff in meetings, of pupils as they moved around a school, of shop windows, boarded-up buildings, school and community noticeboards, school inspection reports, parents meetings, the look of the streets, the makes and condition of cars parked locally, the state of the telephone box, the stray dogs roaming the streets. 'Readings' such as these enable a researcher to 'take a reading' of the setting and to compose a written response to that reading.

Test	Sets tasks in meaningful context	Covers knowledge of environmental print	Covers knowledge of books	Covers writing	Can be repeated	Has a scoring system
Jones and Hendrickson 1970	−	✓	−	−	?	−
Clay 1972	−	−	✓	✓	✓	✓
Thackray & Thackray 1974	−	−	*	−	?	−
Downing & Thackray 1976	−	−	*	−	?	−
Ylisto 1977	✓	✓	−	−	?	✓
Brimer & Raban 1979	−	−	*	−	?	✓
Goodman & Altwerger 1981	−	*	*	*	✓	−
Downing et al. 1983	−	*	*	*	✓	✓
Clymer & Barratt 1983	✓	−	*	−	?	✓
Heibert 1983	✓	−	✓	−	?	−
Goodhall 1984	✓	✓	−	−	✓	−
Manchester 1988	✓	−	✓	✓	✓	−
Barra et al. 1989	✓	−	✓	✓	✓	−
Waterland 1989	✓	−	✓	−	✓	−
Sulzby 1990	✓	−	−	✓	✓	✓
Kent LEA 1992	−	−	*	−	✓	✓
LARR 1993	−	*	*	−	✓	✓
Wandsworth 1994	✓	−	*	*	✓	✓
Desforges Lyndsay 1995	✓	−	*	*	✓	✓
SCAA 1996	✓	−	*	*	✓	✓
Vincent et al. 1996	−	−	*	*	✓	✓
Nutbrown 1997	✓	✓	✓	✓	✓	✓

Key: − no
 * Minimal coverage
 ✓ adequate coverage

Figure 5.7   *Review of measures of literacy in terms of Nutbrown's desirable characteristics*

Source: adapted from Nutbrown 1997 p. 68 and p. 109)

Activity 5.4   'Taking readings'

Read the following two examples of research accounts which derive from 'radical readings' of research settings. After your reading try to note down the various things which the researcher 'read' in order to assemble the account.

Example 1

NICK, PAUL AND ME

In one of the Midlands schools we studied, we spent something like 300 days over two years mainly talking to staff within the scope and schedule of the project. Now this school was of great interest: a big (about 2000 students) place fairly downtown in a big city tired with industrial collapse; fitfully tense – in this retrenchment – with a sub-stantial Pakistani community brought so many years ago thousands of miles indiffer-ently as so many operatives; and made slightly famous by local politicians who polarized each other into caricatures of left and right (one Labour councillor described the Tory leader – in his presence – as "itler wi' knobs on'; this without a smile).

Of a staff of over 140, some eight were employed full time as special educators, mainly supporting children in mainstream classrooms; a further eight worked as lan-guage support teachers with the many students whose first tongue was not English. This is by any standard a high proportion of teachers in support-for-access roles.

I shall tell the whole story elsewhere, but in brief there were many mutterings about these support departments, and in particular about the special needs organi-sation; it was falling apart and was becoming friable as its head of department.

. . .

Few structures held the department together beyond those which organized his own spirit. To be sure, there were timetables, a policy of sorts, schedules for staff to refer children for help. But I insist that these were contingent, mere stuff that routes Nick's energy.

Source: Clough, 1995: 132.

Example 2

I've met my father and his sons in so many Special Schools.

A man I was really frightened of was a miner from Bresswell; he had served in the post-war Army, mainly in Germany, and named his son Klaus in honour and memory, I presume, of a greater life, culture and identity than he enjoyed in this bleak mining village. He had a bayonet over the fireplace. His wife – the mother – had left years before and he had brought Klaus up largely alone with some help from his nearby mother. He was in all respects what would be called, I think, 'a man's man'.

He was five feet eight or so, but broad, and naturally fatty, but strong, too. His face was clearly made to be young – you could see him easily at 20, a sort of Irish look – but had been badly spoiled with hard work, drink and tobacco . . .

. . .

My job was to liaise between home and the special school which Klaus attended in respect of his maladjustment. I made my first visit to the house during the half-term holiday in February. Bresswell is low, somehow; there is a severe grid of council estate painted on top of the slight wold of the east Midland. The miners and their families live over the shop: quite beneath the estate is their work, so these are single story bungalows laid out as Coniston Drive, Langdale Close, Bowness Avenue and so on.

I had written – twice – that I was coming, but there was no sign of life when I arrived at 11. The curtains were drawn at all the windows and this was the only bungalow where there was no smoke from the chimney though this was a February morning. I knocked and banged and I would have gone just as the door opened . . .

Source: Clough, 1996: 75.

Activity 5.5   Taking 'readings' in the field of enquiry

Try 'reading' your own institution, or your morning bus queue or the supermarket. As you reflect on your 'reading' of the situation think about the following:

- What did you 'read'?
- What skills and strategies did you use?
- What assumptions and responses did you make to what you saw?
- How did you make decisions about the meaning of your reading?

Being critical in your own research

This chapter has focused on critical responses to the literature and to the interpretation of research settings. Before we leave the theme of radical reading we want to suggest a final form of critical response to texts and situations in respect of your radical reading of your own research report. Whilst writing your dissertation or thesis, bear in mind the skills of radical reading which you brought to bear on the writing of others and employ these to read your own writing within a critical frame.

Activity 5.6

Revisit the questions to ask the author in Figure 5.3. Respond to them in respect of your own writing.

We shall return to the issue of critical research writing in Chapter 8 which focuses on the research report.

CHAPTER SUMMARY

In this chapter we have:

Defined and demonstrated our view of radical reading in research and argued the importance of radical reading in the research process

Outlined the place of criticality in radical reading of texts and practices

Discussed how research questions can be used to define and refine the focus of a literature search

Demonstrated, through two examples of research, different dimensions of 'radical reading'

Drawn together the practices of radical reading of the texts of others with the need to adopt such a response to your own research writing

📖 FURTHER READING

Hart, C. (1998) *Doing a Literature Review*. London: Sage.

Contains useful ideas and strategies for planning and carrying out a literature search.

Hart, C. (2001) *Doing a Literature Search*. London: Sage.

Contains useful ideas and strategies for planning and writing a good literature review, includes some practical examples.

Pink, S. (2001) *Visual Ethnography*. London: Sage.

This book offers a critical response to 'visual' research methods with some suggestions about analysis and ethical considerations.

6

Questioning: the Focus of Research

CHAPTER CONTENTS

LEARNING OBJECTIVES

By studying and doing the activities in this chapter you will:

◇ have consolidated work covered in Chapter 2 on generating research questions

◇ have reflected on several examples of research involving interviewing and questionnaires

◇ have written a critical response to a section of a research report (which justifies use of questionnaire survey)

◇ have an understanding of the multilayered functions of questions and questioning in research studies

◇ have an awareness of the importance of stating future research questions.

Introduction

> *Radical questioning* reveals not only gaps in knowledge but why and how answers might be morally and politically necessitated. *Radical questioning* lies at the heart of a research study, and brings together the earlier notions of *radically attending* to a topic or situation of events.

In this chapter we shall further develop the idea, introduced in Chapter 2, of *radical questioning*. First we shall reflect on issues already raised in earlier parts of the book in relation to research questions before we move on to discuss the questioning tools often used to collect data – interviews and questionnaires. We follow this discussion with some examples from our own work and from work by our students to demonstrate the use of interviews and questionnaires in the context of the research questions they address. We also note the importance of closing a research report with a statement of further research questions.

Asking questions

We emphasise, in this chapter, the multilayered functions of questions and questioning in research studies; from the generation of research questions, to the decision to ask questions of research participants, to the devising of interview or questionnaire schedules, to questions about the researcher him or herself and the motivation for undertaking the study. In Chapter 2 we suggested that research methodology involves at least three kinds of questions: self-questioning, research questions and field questions. In this chapter we further discuss the functions of these three kinds of questioning. As you will have noted from your reading of earlier chapters, the most important question is 'why?': *why* this topic? *Why* this method? *Why* this setting? *Why* these participants? *Why* this question? These are central questions of *justification* and our reason for investing in *radical questioning* the moral and political roots of research studies.

How to ask – issues of method

In this section we focus on two of the most popular methods for collecting data from research participants: interviews and questionnaires. We shall raise a number of questions to help you to clarify your use of these methods if you choose to use them in your own study.

Interviews

> Asking questions and getting answers is a much harder task
> than it may seem at first. The spoken or written word has
> always a residue of ambiguity, no matter how carefully we
> report or code the answers. Yet interviewing is one of the most
> common and powerful ways in which we try to understand our
> fellow human beings. (Fontana and Frey, 2000: 645)

The first question to ask when considering using interviews to gather data is whether this is the best method for your purposes. You need to think about the kind of data you want, and how much you want to control the interview. You need to decide whether you want to structure the interview so that you set the agenda, whether you simply want to listen to the interviewee's ideas on a particular issue or topic, or whether you want a bit of both. These decisions will influence your later decisions. For example, let us imagine that you want to find out what a sample of the population thinks about children's television. You would need to consider a number of questions. You will need to decide who you are going to interview – this itself generating a number of questions:

- How many people?
- A cross-section of the population?
- A sample of parents of young children?
- People in a particular region of the country or from a number of countries?
- People from a range of cultural and racial groups?
- Men and women?
- Why have you decided to ask adults – why not children?

As you can see, the questions could be endless but, whatever you decide, you need to be able to provide a rationale for those decisions. They must be explained and justified; for example, whether you decide to interview three parents in depth and at length, or 50 people chosen at random in a busy shopping centre very briefly, you must say *why* you made those choices and *how* you selected them for interview.

Then there are more questions:

- Should you produce a schedule with specific questions?
- Should you simply begin turn on a tape recorder and say, 'Could you tell me what you think about children's television?'
- Should you devise an interview schedule which includes some very open questions, such as 'What are your thoughts on children's television?' and more closed

questions such as 'How much television do you think 3-year-olds should be allowed to watch?'

These and many other questions, and the resolution of them, will depend on the reason for your carrying out the study, your research question or questions, and the extent to which you want the ideas of research participants to emerge from the study and influence its direction.

It is always good practice to pilot your interview ideas first with a small number of people who are similar to your sample. Try out your equipment, your technique, your questions and your ability to probe further, and then ask the interviewees to tell you how the interview felt for them, whether they understood the questions, whether you could have done anything else to obtain better data. It is important to remember that the actual interview can generate a large amount of data.

If you tape record interviews, by far the best way to obtain the actual words interviewees have used, you may find that a tape of a 45-minute interview takes up to seven hours to transcribe! Few students have the facility of secretarial services to transcribe audio recordings, so it will be important to think about how you will extract responses from a tape and how you will use all the data collected. Collecting data is one challenge but (as we see in Chapter 7) making sense of the growing amounts of data is often the greater challenge!

The equipment needed to tape a telephone interview is easily obtainable and inexpensive; you simply need a cable to connect your telephone to the tape recorder. You must also tell the interviewee that you are recording them! This is also a relatively inexpensive way to collect data. Telephone; video conferencing and the internet make it possible to interview people who live some distance away without the expense of travel.

Activity 6.1   Thinking about your interviewees – justifying decisions

Imagine you are planning a project which involves you interviewing parents and young children about their views on television programmes for young children.

Consider how you would approach the interviews of both children and parents. You may need to ask yourself a series of questions such as:

- Do I interview children and parents together or separately?
- Do I interview children in small groups – hold a kind of focus group?
- How many parents should I interview?
- Where should I interview the children?
- Where should I interview the parents?
- What should I ask children?
- What should I ask parents?

Write about 300–400 words which list the questions you need to ask yourself and how you would resolve them. Make sure you know *why* you make the decisions you do; for example, why would you decide to interview six parents instead of 25? This is the important element of methodology, the justification of your research decisions.

Devising interview questions

Having made those crucial research decisions about whether to interview and who, the task then is to devise the interview questions and make decisions about the style and tone of the interview. We can best discuss this through a recent example of our own work. In 2000 and again in 2001, as part of our own research at the University of Sheffield, we interviewed five teachers who were working in schools using the *Index for Inclusion* (Booth et al., 2000).

The first set of interviews in March 2000 were carried out face to face; the second set of interviews – following up the experience some 14 months later – was done by telephone using the schedule in Figure 6.1. The questions are fairly open, designed to elicit teachers' responses, asking them to address the issues on which we were trying to focus. The teachers were sent the interview schedule beforehand so that they were familiar with the questions and could, if they wished, prepare their responses. The schedule *guided* the interview but did not *dictate* the path. That is to say, if there were other issues the teachers wanted to raise they were encouraged to do so. (This decision relates to the discussion on 'voice' in Chapter 4). Data collection took some eight hours in total, but it took an experienced secretary using a transcribing machine more than 30 hours to produce transcripts of all five telephone interviews. Transcripts were then sent to the interviewees for amendment before any analysis was begun. Figure 6.1 shows the interview schedule we used. The bold headings being the categories we planned to adopt at the first level of analysis.

We will turn to the final report of this piece of research later in this chapter but first we want to focus on the questions themselves.

What do I do when I've done my interviews?

Once you have carried out your interviews you have a wealth of data which you must process and analyse. In fact, you must generate another set of questions with which to interrogate the data. There are many ways to do this but, however you approach the task, you need to ensure that you are remaining true to the voices of the research participants and developing responses to your research questions. You will need to become familiar with your interview transcripts and notes, get a 'feel' for the data and perhaps create an overview of what people have told you – your

Name..

School..

Telephone number..

Email...

Date of interview...

[name] ... thanks for agreeing to talk to us again. As you know we're interested in what has happened in your school since you've been using the Index for Inclusion. There are just five questions, and perhaps there may be other things you want to add. So shall we begin with the first? I'll jot down some notes while we're talking but I'll also record the interview, so I'll turn on the tape now, OK? Let's begin.

1   **You first saw the *Index for Inclusion* when it was launched in March 2000. What were your first impressions of the *Index*?**

2   **Now you've been working with it for 14 months. Did the *Index* change your practice?**

3   **What about other changes? Did using the *Index* change your thinking?**

4   **In the time you've been using it: what have you learned by working with the *Index*?**

5   **My last question: would you recommend the *Index* to other early childhood education settings?**

Thanks, [name] is there anything else you want to say about the *Index*, or working with it?

We really appreciate your help with this study. We will send you the transcript in the next week

Figure 6.1   *Interview schedule: Index for Inclusion*
Source: (Nutbrown and Clough, 2002)

Activity 6.2

We wanted to find out about the personal experiences of people using the *Index for Inclusion*; the impact on their work and on their thinking. We needed short prompts to make sure that we did not forget important things during the telephone calls. We also needed space to make brief notes as the interview proceeded. Look through the questions in the interview schedule.

Do you think they actually did generate the data we needed? What about the introductory words and the closing statement?

If you use interviews, think about the design of your own interview schedule. Do the questions you ask help you to respond to your research questions? Does the schedule itself enable you to conduct the interview (whether by telephone or face to face) appropriately?

Make some notes in your research journal of the things you need to remember when you are designing an interview schedule.

Interviewing: some hints

Do your interview questions help you to respond to your research questions?

Have you carried out a pilot run of your interview schedule?

Make sure the questions are clear

Generating data is easy!

Get parents' permission to interview pupils in schools

Give people time to respond – don't rush

Make it easy for interviewees to respond

Listen

Tape-record your interviews

Test your equipment before each interview

Think about the arrangement of the room and seating – make sure interviewees feel comfortable

Tell participants why you are interviewing them

'impressions' and 'intuitions' (we shall return to this theme in Chapter 7). You will perhaps want to draw together comments on a particular theme, or you may wish to collate the very different responses to the same question. You may want to use a quantitative approach to analyse some of the data, counting up how many people said 'x' or how many said 'y', though of course this will depend on the research questions and on the number of people in your sample. Quantitative responses to the data in our study (Nutbrown and Clough, 2002, reported later in this chapter) would be quite inappropriate for two reasons: the small sample and the focus of the research. If you do decide to carry out some quantitative analysis there are now a number of computer packages which you can use. This may or may not be a useful way to proceed if it suits your study. You may be able to add up the various responses yourself and draw meaning from it without the use of a statistical package. You will find helpful suggestions in the chapter on Interviews by Cohen, Manion and Morrison (2000: Ch. 15).

Interviewing: an example

One of the best ways to learn about the appropriate use of various methods is to read journal articles which report research carried out using the methods in which you are interested. We have included here an article we wrote in 2002, which uses interview data collected both in person and using the telephone. We suggest that you first read the article and then try the activity which follows it.

THE INDEX FOR INCLUSION:

PERSONAL PERSPECTIVES FROM EARLY YEARS EDUCATORS

Cathy Nutbrown and Peter Clough
The University of Sheffield, School of Education

> *Respectful educators will include all children; not just children who are easy to work with, obliging, endearing, clean, pretty, articulate, capable, but every child – respecting them for who they are, respecting their language, their culture, their history, their family, their abilities, their needs, their name, their ways and their very essence.*
>
> (Nutbrown 1996 p 54)

The *Index for Inclusion* was launched in March 2000 and a copy was issued to every State school in England. Developed by eminent leaders in the field of inclusion, the *Index* maps out a process designed to lead to radical change through the development of learning and participation of all involved in the life of a school (Booth *et al.* 2000). For some schools the *Index* has proved to be precisely the tool for development which they were seeking, whilst for others it has become just another ring-binder housed on a shelf full of such ring-binders: full of good ideas, viewed with good intentions, 'if only we had the time'.

Arising from a number of research projects during the last two years, we have become very interested in the reaction of early childhood professionals to the *Index* and how it influenced their personal responses to issues of inclusion. In this article we draw on interviews with five early years practitioners to examine the concept of Inclusion in general and their response to the *Index* in particular. We interviewed five practitioners in March 2000 and again (fourteen months later) in July 2001 after they had used the *Index*. This is a small study which focuses on the *experience* of participants, thus uncovering those personal reflections which, though they often inform the outcomes of larger evaluations, are less frequently reported. We are seeking here not to evaluate the *Index for Inclusion*, but rather to report the experience of a small number of people who have worked with it.

Why are we talking about 'inclusion'?

Constructions of difference and difficulty

It has been argued that Early Education at its best *is* Inclusive Education (Nutbrown 1998), because it is often the experience of those who work within the Foundation Stage that children with learning difficulties and/or disabilities are included *as a first option*. In such settings we would argue that Inclusion is as much about *attitude* as it is about *response?*

Educators, managers of settings and parents (among others) make decisions about children and their difficulties, and behind every decision made in response to an instance of educational difficulty, there lie traditions of practice that more or less evidently affect outcomes. As Herbert demonstrates in the case of Steven:

> 'This was the first time in her short career that Steven's reception class teacher had had a child with a statement in her class. She was conscious that by choosing the inclusive option Steven's parents had accepted that he needed to interact with his peer group and not become, once more, dependent upon adults. She was reassured by the head that it was not a scenario of 'success or failure' and was given support to evaluate her own practice in a way which led her to believe that her established skills of providing a well structured and stimulating learning environment for all children were particularly relevant for Steven. She realised that it was her duty to attend not only to what was 'special' about Steven but also to what was 'ordinary' and that there was no mystique to analysing tasks. She was already doing this and making them accessible to all children, including children with learning difficulties'.

(Herbert, 1998, p. 103)

The decisions made by parents and teachers in the case discussed above by Herbert pointed to an outcome of *inclusive* practice. How an individual educator, an early years setting, a local authority or service *constructs* both a problem and its solution is determined by their characteristic habits of interpretation. In the example above, Herbert draws attention to the transferable skills of a teacher of five-year-olds to 'analyse skills' and present learning situations to children in ways which fit their own individual needs. It goes without saying that other interpretations may well be made, dependent upon experience and upon cultural determinants.

Roots of Inclusion: routes to inclusion

It is worth taking a moment to consider how we have come to use the term 'Inclusion' and to explore the roots of our present policy response to the education of young children with a variety of curricular, physical, emotional and social needs.

Inclusive ideology and practice has emerged – in only 50 years – from within a situation of statutory, categorical exclusion. *Special education itself has been transformed from the outside* by civilising forces which have deconstructed and reconstructed its meanings and effects. The move – from segregated Special Education in special schools, to Integration and the development of 'units' within schools, to Inclusion of pupils in 'mainstream' settings – has been fuelled by the various ideologies and perspectives which marked their 'moments' in history (Clough 1998). It is possible to sketch out a rough history of the development of inclusive education which identifies five major perspectives (Figure 1). Though never wholly exclusive of each other they demonstrate historical influences which shape, in part, current views and practices.

By looking 'back' through the disability studies critique of the 1990s at influences of the psycho-medical model, the sociological response, curricular approaches and school improvement measures, is it possible to look *forward* to the emergence of a more homogeneous response to inclusive education where individual children's *rights* to inclusive education (as well as *needs for* individually appropriate education) – are at centre stage *from the start of their educational career*. Looking back we can see how tests, labels and deficits dominated the identification of children's learning needs – a legacy from the psycho-medical model dominant in the 50s. As Sebba and Sachdev (1997) point out, educational 'labels' rather than categorisation 'labels' (for example: 'reading difficulties' rather than 'Down's Syndrome') lead to more inclusive responses to children's learning needs. In the move towards inclusive education, recent developments have hinted at a convergence of thinking about inclusion and about how best this can be achieved. The *Index for Inclusion* is one example of such convergence, an outcome of a particularly fruitful collaboration which is designed to help schools understand what they *mean* by inclusion as well as to identify their inclusive practices and blocks to those practices.

The psycho-medical legacy (1950s ⇨)

This is understood as the system of broadly medicalized ideas which essentially saw the *individual* as being somehow 'in deficit' and in turn assumed a need for a 'special' education for those individuals.

The sociological response (1960s ⇨)

This position broadly represents the critique of the 'psycho-medical legacy', and draws attention to a social *construction* of special educational needs.

Curricular approaches (1970s ⇨)

Such approaches emphasise the role of the *curriculum* in both meeting – and, for some writers, effectively *creating* – learning difficulties.

School improvement strategies (1980s ⇨)

This movement emphasises the importance of systematic organization in pursuit of truly *comprehensive* schooling.

Disability studies critique (1990s ⇨)

These perspectives, often from 'outside' education, elaborate an overtly political response to the exclusionary effects of the psycho-medical model

Figure 1   *Five key perspectives on educational inclusion*

Source: Clough 2000 p.8

Perspectives on Inclusion

From the 'academy' . . .

> Some continue to want to make inclusion primarily about 'special needs education' or the inclusion in education of children and young people with impairments but that position seems absurd ... If inclusion is about the development of comprehensive community education and about prioritising community over individualism beyond education, then the history of inclusion is the history of these struggles for an education system which serves the interests of communities and which does not exclude anyone within those communities.

(Booth 2000 p.64)

Tony Booth's position here, then, is that inclusive education is about education for *all* members of the community – all minority and oppressed groups. From this broad definition of inclusion it could be argued that *Sure Start* initiatives and *Early Excellence Centres* are – in effect – projects of Inclusion in the Early Years.

From practitioners . . .

We asked five early childhood educators what they meant by the term *inclusion*. Here they talk about their own understanding of inclusion and what their settings do to develop inclusive practice.

> *It's about letting children with Special Educational Needs come to the school in their neighbourhood. I think that's right, but it doesn't always work out.*
>
> Kay
> Nursery Nurse
> Nursery Centre 2–5 years

> *It's political. It's about social justice – giving every child the right to an education in their own community – which enables them to reach their full potential. For me, that means doing a lot of work to make sure that the staff here is aware – but also arguing for resources. Managing that is a challenge. The greatest need is for personal awareness – so I need money for staff development – installing ramps is easy – changing attitudes – challenging prejudice – that's the real issue of inclusion – it is a huge issue.*
>
> Sue
> Head Teacher
> School 3–10 years

> *Well, I think inclusion is really about equality. About not shutting children out. If children are kept out of the system at this stage they'll always be different – seen as different. It's easy to say that though – not always so easy to include children – especially some who are very disruptive. Children with disabilities aren't a problem – I don't worry about them – they usually fit in well – toilets are a problem sometimes but we get round that! It's children who can't behave – can't fit into the group – mess up the equipment, slop paint everywhere – throw things – bite – I tear my hair out over them. They're the ones that are in danger of exclusion and being separated off at 5 years old – that's terrible isn't it? But I can't help it – I have to survive, and I have to think about the rest of the children.*
>
> Helen
> Reception Class Teacher
> School 3–7 years

> *A lovely idea – inclusion – and when it's good, it's great! I have been able to have children in the nursery with Down's Syndrome and children with various emotional difficulties – abused children – but when they (the LEA) asked us to take in a child with Autism, well, we had to say 'no'. Too risky – I was frightened that if we did – something terrible would happen and it would be my responsibility. So yes, lovely idea – but it really is an ideal that will never be achieved – total inclusion is impossible.*
>
> Janie
> Nursery Teacher
> School 3–10 years

*I spend my life arguing for extra support for children with SEN who we're trying
to keep in our school rather than send them to 'Special'. Inclusion of all children
in the community would be so much easier if it were the norm – the first resort
– that's usually the case in the nursery, but as children go on into school that
philosophy seems to fade and the first move seems to be 'how can I get rid of
this one'*

Pauline
SENCO
School 3–10 years

So, how typical are these voices on inclusion? To what extent can the political ideal
of social justice be realised in practice in the early years of education? How far are
these *ideals of equity* and *fears of risk* shared by early childhood educators generally?
A recently published 'snapshot of practice' includes many examples of work with
children with special educational needs in the early years (Wolfendale 2000). This
collection demonstrates the diversity of experience and attitude towards *needs* and
to the concept of *inclusion*. Wolfendale presents many positive accounts of including
young children with identified learning needs in nurseries or other early education
settings; but there is another side to the coin – as our interviewees alert. The failure
of inclusion hurts; Nutbrown (1998) gives an account of a nursery teacher who,
reluctantly, tried to include a child with Autism into her nursery; things went badly
wrong because of endemic difficulties within the setting itself:

*Martin was admitted to a nursery full of children with damage and dislocation
in their lives – physical and sexual abuse, overwhelming poverty, disproportion-
ate ill-health, numerous wet beds, and no end of broken hearts.*

*Martin stayed for two weeks. Each day his teacher talked with his mother.
Each day she told her what Martin had enjoyed, and of the struggle he had with
his peers in the nursery. There were many troubled children in Martin's company, and though Martin was interested, bright and he was able, the nursery disabled him. In that setting he was not being included in a calm, ordered society.
He was not a member of a predictable community, he was appended into a
community of children and adults in chaos.*

*After two weeks Martin left. His teacher hoped he had not been harmed, but
she knew the harm it had caused his mother. Martin went to a nursery a few
miles away which had a special unit for children with special educational needs
and which worked to include children from that unit into mainstream classes
once they had become established in the school community.*

(Nutbrown 1998 p. 170)

Martin's story is a warning that early years settings must be fit to include, and
educators equipped with appropriate professional development and management
support. Berry's (2001) study of four children indicates that inclusion *can* work for
some children and the factors for success depend upon the children's responses as

well as those of educators and parents and on the ability of the adults so involved to listen, really listen, to the children's voices.

How do we know inclusion when we see it?

The *Index for Inclusion* is a tool for school development. It is summarised as follows:

> The *Index* is a set of materials to guide schools through a process of inclusive school development. It is about building supportive communities which foster high achievement for all students. The process of using the *Index* is itself designed to contribute to the inclusive development of schools. It encourages staff to share and build on existing knowledge and assists them in a detailed examination of the possibilities for increasing learning and participation for all their students.
>
> The *Index* involves a process of school self-review on three dimensions concerned with inclusive school cultures, policies and practices. The process entails progression through a series of school development phases. These start with the establishing of a co-ordinating group. This group works with staff, governors, students and parents/carers to examine all aspects of the school, identifying barriers to learning and sustaining and reviewing progress. The investigation is supported by a detailed set of indicators and questions which require schools to engage in a deep, and challenging exploration of their present position and the possibilities for moving towards greater inclusion.
>
> (Index for Inclusion 2000 p.2)

So, the index is intended to enable schools to 'sample' their cultures, policies and practices to see how they measure up to the view of inclusion articulated above by Tony Booth, a view which embraces inclusion of *all*, and addresses aspects of gender, class, race, religion, sexuality, social class as much as learning difficulty or disability.

Of course, we know from our research that some early childhood settings and providers have not encountered the *Index*. Because of the diversity of provision, some – non-school – settings may well have missed the launch of the *Index* and have not (as yet) been able to work with it, nor judge its usefulness to their setting. The *Index* is not 'just' about SEN and is distinct from statutory frameworks and structures such as the SEN code of Practice 2001 (see Roffey 2001 for discussion of the legal context).

Using the Index for Inclusion

Some Local Education Authorities and some schools have used the *Index for Inclusion* to great effect as an instrument of school change (Clough and Corbett 2000). But we were interested in how the *Index* made a difference to individual professional responses to inclusion; we wanted to know whether using the *Index* affected the personal 'routes to inclusion' of early childhood educators. After they had used the *Index* in their own schools and centres we returned to the five early years practitioners and asked them to reflect on their experience, and to talk about their own learning. We asked them five questions:

---

1 What were your first impressions of the *Index*?
2 Did the *Index* change your practice?
3 Did using the *Index* change your thinking?
4 What have you learned by working with the *Index*?
5 Would you recommend the *Index* to other early childhood education settings?

Here is a flavour of their responses:

Fantastic – a real eye opener. I never thought about some of the dimensions as being part of inclusive practice. I realise how inclusive we are! Of parents, of children from ethnic minority groups – It made me think – 'Am I being inclusive – as a professional?' Yes – I've really learned quite a bit – about me and my own attitudes – and about what other people who work here know too – and have shared.

Kay
Nursery Nurse
Nursery Centre 2–5 years

It suggests setting up a co-ordinating group. That's important for large schools – but it works equally well in small settings where there are not large numbers of staff. We used it in a series of staff meetings. Got the children as well as staff to do questionnaires. It really raised awareness, amongst staff, children and also with parents. My Governors were interested too – even when it came to spending money! There's very good practice – and positive will – it is such an effective process – takes some sustaining though! We were encouraged to realise that we had many aspects of inclusive culture and our main task was to extend and develop what we did.

Sue
Head Teacher
School 3–10 years

When they said we were going to do this I thought 'another initiative in another glossy folder'. I was sceptical – I admit – I wondered what the point was of doing another audit when we could have spent the time and money on a part time support assistance for my class. But it was interesting – made me think – but whether it will make a difference in the end – well, we'll see.

Helen
Reception Class Teacher
School 3–7 years

I learned loads just by reading through the folder – thinking about the questions posed under the different dimensions – there's so much to think about – mind-blowing! It's a process that's never actually finished – but it feels very good. It is really about developing relationships – that's what it's about – valuing people enough to make relationships with them and then finding ways of working in that richness of diversity.

Janie
Nursery Teacher
School 3–10 years

He (the Head) said 'We should do this – take it home and see what you think'. As I worked through it, it all made sense – cultures, policies and practice – really obvious but it had to be laid out for us. So I took the folder back and said 'Yes – good idea – we should do this'. And the Head said 'Great! Will you set up the group?' It's been a lot of work but getting the children involved and the parents was really good – made a difference to the way we think about things now – I think. I would say that we're – most of us – at the point where we 'think' inclusion now – first.

Pauline
SENCO
School 3–10 years

We have been at pains here to let the voices of those people we interviewed speak for themselves, to convey – largely unedited – their experiences, excitements and reservations. In conclusion we return to our five questions and ask why the index is necessary.

Why do we need an Index?

It seems that it is not uncommon to greet yet another development initiative with scepticism; as Helen said: *'another initiative in another glossy folder'*. Yet the five people we spoke to have conveyed something of a personal response to the *Index* which suggests a change *in themselves*. We are left with the impression that there is a great deal of personal interrogation, personal learning, personal change which results as an outcome of engaging with the index. As Pauline says: *we 'think' inclusion now*. Can such changes in thinking, in attitude, in realisation fail to result in changes in practice? If our five participants are in any way typical we have something to learn about the capacity of the *Index* to bring about personal/professional change. As Kay told us:

That whole idea that 'Inclusion' isn't just the latest PC term for SEN – that was really refreshing.

A key point in the interviews was the development of a shared language for discussion. Sue commented: *'We've got a language now to discuss things within the school'* and this change in language resulted in Pauline negotiating a change in her title as Special Educational Need Co-ordinator: *I've asked to be called the 'Learning Support Co-ordinator' now. It doesn't really fit, being a SENCO, in an inclusive school!*

Their work with the *Index* in their settings, they told us, made a difference to them as individuals. It was not always easy, as Helen admitted: *It was painful at times. I had to confront and admit some personal prejudices.* But it seems that these early childhood professionals would want to recommend the *Index for Inclusion* to others, in other settings so that they can find out for themselves.

'It's not something you can get second hand,
you have to be part of the thinking, part of the change'

Acknowledgements

We would like to thank Kay, Sue, Helen, Janie and Pauline for sharing their experiences and perspectives with us. Thanks also to Sue Webster for her comments on an earlier draft of this article.

References

BERRY, T. (2001) 'Does inclusion work? A case study of four children', unpublished MA in Early Childhood Education dissertation. Sheffield: University of Sheffield

BOOTH, T. AINSCOW, M. BLACK-HAWKINS, K. VAUGHAN, M. SHAW, L. (2000) *Index for Inclusion: developing learning and participation in schools* Bristol: Centre for Studies in Inclusive Education. The *Index* is available from: CSIE 1 Redland Close, Elm Lane, Redland, Bristol BS6 6UE

BOOTH, T. (2000) Reflection. In P. Clough and J. Corbett (2000) *Theories of Inclusive Education: a students' guide* London: PCP/SAGE

CLOUGH, P (ed) (1998) *Managing Inclusive Education: From Policy to Experience* London PCP/SAGE

CLOUGH, P. (2000) Routes to inclusion. In P. Clough and J. Corbett (2000) *Theories of Inclusive Education* London: PCP/SAGE

HERBERT, E. (1988) Included from the street? Managing Early Years Settings for All. In P. Clough (ed.) *Managing Inclusive Education: From Policy to Experience* London: PCP/SAGE

NUTBROWN, C (1998) Managing to Include? Rights, responsibilities and respect. In P. Clough (ed) *Managing Inclusive Education: From Policy to Experience* London PCP/SAGE

NUTBROWN, C (ed) (1996) *Respectful Educators: Capable Learners – children's rights and Early Education* London: PCP/SAGE

ROFFEY, S. (2001) *Special Needs in the Early Years: collaboration, communication and coordination* (2nd Edn) London: David Fulton

SEBBA, J. and SACHDEV, D. (1997) *What works in Inclusive Education?* Ilford: Barnardo's

WOLFENDALE, S. (ed) (2000) *Special Needs in the Early Years: Snapshots of Practice* London: RoutledgeFalmer

Source: This article was first published in *Early Education* – the Journal of the British Association for Early Childhood Education – in January 2002. It is reproduced here with permission.

Activity 6.3

Having read this article, list the questions you would want to ask Nutbrown and Clough about this piece of research.
   Do you think they chose the right method to collect the data?
   Were they justified in selecting a small number of people to interview?
   How else might such a study have been designed?

Questionnaire

> The questionnaire is a widely used and useful instrument for collecting survey information, providing structured, often numerical data, being able to be administered without the presence of the researcher, and often being comparatively straightforward to analyse . . . These attractions have to be counterbalanced by the time taken to develop, pilot and refine the questionnaire, by the possible unsophistication and limited scope of the data that are collected, and from the likely limited flexibility of response. (Cohen, Manion and Morrison, 2000: 245)

Generally speaking, questionnaires allow researchers to survey a population of subjects, with little or no personal interaction, and with the aim of establishing a broad picture of their experiences or views. The important term here is *broad*, for it is unlikely that a questionnaire will reveal the *depth* of those views and experiences in any of their rich detail. This distinction is essentially what separates qualitative and quantitative approaches to enquiry, and in Chapter 7 we pursue that distinction at greater length. Here, however, we are concerned with what any and all research methods have in common in their generation of radical questioning.

   Questionnaire methods are at the 'hard' – the arguably more scientific – end of the spectrum of social science enquiry. Perhaps more than any other method of enquiry in social science, there are techniques of questionnaire design which are not specific to given topics but which apply across all instances of use. These concern procedures for such as the construction of questions, the anticipation of a frame of analysis, and claims to significance. In these and other cases, there are some well-understood and accepted rules of design and administration of questionnaires (see Cohen, Manion and Morrison, 2000: 245); the examination of how these rules have been observed – that is, in terms of reliability, validity and so on – are key features of a qualitative methodology. The significance of the large-scale study which seeks to create *generalisations* from its data rests crucially on its observance of these rules.

However, the most important of these rules are reflected in small-scale studies, too, even where generalisation is not an aim. Although they are not applied – and 'policed' – in the same detail, many of these same rules are to be found implicitly in a persuasive research account, whatever methods it employs. This is because its methodology – its *claim to significance* – addresses the same radical questions which are made more technically explicit in the quantitative study. These are:

What are my research questions?
What sort of – and how much – information do I need to answer my research questions?
What field questions do I need to ask to get this information?
What method/s should I use to pose these field questions?

These are questions which can be applied to all methods; what really matters, then, in choosing to use a questionnaire is the precise understanding of what it can and cannot reveal in terms of the central research questions.

Questionnaires: some examples

In this section we draw on two studies, carried out by our former students, to illustrate how questionnaires can be used to generate data in research. The first, by Al Kaddah (2001) examined students' motivation for learning English as a Second Language; and the second (Raymond, 2001) explored students' perceptions of 'excellent teaching'. A brief overview is given of each study followed by the authors' rationale for using questionnaires.

Example 1: Motivation and learning a second language

Discussing the aims of her study Al Kaddah states that she wanted to explore the 'social, historical and cultural factors that affected the motivation to learn English of students at a women's tertiary college in the United Arab Emirates (UAE)'. Al Kaddah surveyed different students at three stages in their three year course; she also carried out some follow-up interviews to explore further the issues arising from the questionnaire survey, she summarises her approach some of the methodological issues:

> My research took the form of a case study. Data was collected by questionnaire survey and follow-up interviews. Students in Terms 2, 8 and 10 of a twelve-term Diploma course were surveyed; that is, at three separate points within their three-year course. This made it possible to explore the differences in motivational factors at different points of the program. The information was gathered using self-completion questionnaires, the use of standard questions making it possible to draw comparisons between responses. As with the work of Schmidt *et al* (1996), a variety of concepts were examined tentatively rather than a few concepts thoroughly.

The questionnaires asked respondents to indicate the degree to which they agreed or disagreed with a list of statements and to provide a small amount of biographical information. Pilot interviews using an interview schedule were carried out to 'explore the origins, complexities, and ramifications of the attitude areas in question,' and to elicit, 'vivid expressions of such attitudes from the respondents, in a form that might make them suitable for use as statements in an attitude scale' (Oppenheim, 1992: 178). The language used was as simple as possible and the questionnaires for Term 2 were translated into Arabic, as the students' level of English was not as advanced as those of the students in terms 8 and 10. I piloted the questionnaires with a term 4 class to check that students were able to understand and respond to the questionnaire without difficulty.

This study was, in effect, a 'mapping exercise' rather than a measuring exercise and, as a result, attitudes were identified and explored rather than measured or assessed. As such, I chose not to score responses but to analyse them qualitatively.

A pilot questionnaire was trialled with a group of my students and, as a result of that trial, the questionnaire was significantly added to in order to reach the final form. After obtaining necessary permissions the questionnaires were distributed to the English speaking teachers of the classes chosen (with a covering letter explaining the purpose and instructions for completion). I chose to ask English teachers to distribute the questionnaires because they were in a position to help with any language problems the students might have had in completing the questionnaires. This also overcame one of the problems of non-response, as it was made easy for the teachers to administer and return the questionnaires and many expressed their support for this research. Students could choose not to fill in the questionnaire and whether or not to add their name. (Al Kaddah, 2001: 35–6)

In the above extract Al Kaddah explains why certain decisions taken in the development and distribution of her questionnaires were necessary to the execution of the study. She justifies changes to the questionnaire following the pilot, the use of Arabic for relatively new students and English for students in the latter half of their course and the use of other teaching colleagues to distribute the questionnaires.

Example 2: *Excellent teaching – perceptions of Arab, Chinese and Canadian students*

In her study Raymond (2001) sought to 'identify, describe and analyse the characteristics of exemplary post-secondary teachers as perceived by Chinese, Arab and Canadian students'. Raymond surveyed 150 ESL/EFL first-year post-secondary students and used quantitative and qualitative methods to analyse the data generated to respond to the following research questions:

1 Are there differences amongst Arab, Chinese and Canadian students in their perceptions of characteristics associated with excellent teaching?
2 Are there universal attributes associated with exemplary teachers, regardless of differing cultural backgrounds?
3 Do Arab, Chinese and Canadian students have different preferred learning styles?
4 How do Arab, Chinese and Canadian students independently rank, in order of importance, a number of characteristics associated with teaching?
5 Is the notion of the excellent teacher culture bound? That is, is it limited to one country? (Raymond, 2001: 19)

In her summary of methodological issues Raymond states that:

This was a descriptive study using multi-method research procedures with both quantitative and qualitative components. Data were collected in order to accurately describe characteristics of exemplary teachers from the customers themselves (the students). The sample population was drawn from 150 ESL/EFL first-year post secondary students and distributed equally to three distinct cultural groups: Arab, Chinese and Canadian. The characteristics of the excellent teacher as perceived by these three groups of fifty students were assessed through a researcher-designed, field-tested questionnaire instrument. The self-reported survey instrument consisted of twenty-five closed-choice questions and one open-ended question. In addition, recorded interviews were conducted with a sample from each population group.

I collected the data, examined it for usability and entered details into an MS Excel spreadsheet. Bar charts and tables were constructed for analysis.

Scoring of each questionnaire item by each population group was ranked by descending order. Using the data generated by the questionnaire, the top five and bottom five scored items were identified and analyzed. The quantitative data were displayed in tables and charts and accompanied by narrative text.

The qualitative data from the open-ended question and interview questions were categorized into ten emergent themes and entered into sub-categories. Frequency counts were determined and the emergent themes were ranked in descending order by population group. This data was then displayed in tables and charts, and accompanied by narrative text.

Statistical analyses such as ANOVA, Chi Square, or Standard Deviation were not applied to any of these data. For future research purposes statistical analyses of the data would yield a more scientific, accurate interpretation of the data. (Raymond, 2001: 4)

In both of the above examples, various methodological decisions are reported and justified. They are designed to persuade the reader that questionnaires – in the context of the given studies – were the right tools for this particular research purpose.

Activity 6.4

If you are considering carrying out a questionnaire survey in your own research, think about the summary you might write to explain and justify your decision. Try writing it in your research journal – use some of the factors discussed in the two preceding accounts as prompts for your own.

Questionnaires: some hints

Do the field questions help you to respond to your research questions?

Have you carried out a pilot run of your questionnaire?

Are the questions clear? (you will not be there to clarify them)

Are you excluding any participants by requiring a particular level of literacy?

Questionnaires can quickly generate a large amount of data. Do you know how you will use it?

Make it easy to respond: include a stamped addressed envelope.

Think about offering anonymity.

Set a timescale for returns.

Questionnaires may well be a quick way to generate large amounts of data, but they can take some time to design so that the responses received are of the kind you hope for, and the questions are clear to the respondent. Nutbrown and Hannon (1997) carried out a questionnaire survey of 25 teachers to ask their views on a theoretical framework which they had developed in a research project focusing on work with parents on children's early literacy development (see Nutbrown and Hannon, 1996). The questionnaire was piloted by three teachers who were not part of the sample, revised and then sent out by post to the teachers to be surveyed. A report of the study is available (Nutbrown and Hannon, 1997) but at this point we are interested in the design of the questionnaire which follows on pages 123–126.

During the REAL Project Seminars held at the start of the Project we have been discussing and working with the ORIM Framework. We have considered various strands of literacy:

- Environmental Print,
- Book Sharing,
- Early Writing

and

- Developing Language for Literacy.

We have asked four main questions in relation to each of these strands:

- How can we help parents provide **OPPORTUNITIES**?
- How can we enhance parents' **RECOGNITION** of early achievement?
- How can we support/extend parents' **INTERACTION** with their children?
- Can we suggest how parents could provide a **MODEL**?

Having shared some of our ideas with you throughout the Seminars we now want to evaluate the usefulness of the ORIM framework for work with parents and their young children. We need to know whether to modify the framework, drop it, or stick with it. Your views can help us decide. Please answer each of the questions on the inside pages and write any further comments on the back page.

Please return this completed questionnaire in the SAE provided to: Cathy Nutbrown, REAL Project Office, Education Building, University of Sheffield, 388 Glossop Road, Sheffield, S10 2JA

It would be helpful if you could return your completed questionnaire before 12th July – but better later than never!

1 Does the idea of different strands of literacy make sense?   Yes [   ] No [   ]

Please explain your answer.

---

2 Have you found the ORIM framework to be a useful way of thinking about the things parents do to promote children's literacy?   Yes [   ] No [   ]

If yes, in what way?

---

3 Has ORIM changed the way you think about early literacy development and work with parents?   Yes [   ] No [   ]

Can you say how?

---

4 Looking at children's literacy, can you think of any other aspects of the parent's role you might add to the framework (in addition to Opportunities, Recognition, Interaction and Model)?   Yes [   ] No [   ]

Could you give an example and say why you think these additional aspects are important?

---

5 Are there any of the four elements (Opportunities, Recognition, Interaction, Model) that you disagree with or would like further clarification of?

     Yes [   ] No [   ]

If yes, please say which and, if possible, what is unclear or wrong.

6 Has the ORIM Framework helped you in your work with parents?

Yes [   ] No [   ] Partly [   ]

7 Have you, in the past, made use of any other practical frameworks or guidelines in any work with parents and children on early literacy?

Yes [   ] No [   ] Partly [   ]

Please give some details of what you have used.

8 If you were explaining ORIM to someone new to the idea, what would you say was its main value?

9 Similarly, if asked to be critical, what are the main disadvantages or weaknesses of ORIM?

10 If you plan future work with parents will you use the ORIM framework?

Yes [   ] No [   ]

Please explain the reason for your answer.

Please use this page to continue or for further comments if you wish.

One last question:
Which REAL Project Seminars did you attend? Please tick
1. Introduction [   ]
2. Environmental Print [   ]
3. Sharing Books [   ]
4. Early Writing [   ]
5. Developing Language for Literacy [   ]
6. Parents as Adult Learners [   ]

We may wish to talk with you further about some of your responses and ideas. It will be useful to us to know who has given which responses so we have included your name and address below. If you wish to return an anonymous questionnaire please remove or delete the label. If the information is incorrect please let us know. Whilst we may quote from the responses we will not attribute them to named individuals or schools.

Name and address of respondent

Thank you. Your co-operation can help make the Project more effective.

Activity 6.5   Critiquing questionnaires

Look at the questionnaire on pages 123–126 devised by Nutbrown and Hannon (1997) then write a sentence or two in response to the following questions:

- Are the questions phrased in helpful ways?
- Do they make it easy for respondents to give negative responses?
- Does the design make response easy?
- How would you respond to the request from researchers to complete such a questionnaire?
- Do you think a questionnaire was the best tool to use to obtain the kind of data needed for the study?

Make some notes on what you have learned about questionnaire design which will be useful in your own research.

In this section we have discussed the use of interviews and questionnaires as a research tool. The examples provided in this chapter have been chosen to help you reflect on the use of interviews and questionnaires in your own research, and of the need to justify these as the 'right' research decisions for the studies under discussion.

Activity 6.6

If you are planning to use either interviews or questionnaires to collect data you may wish to write your own summary of the usefulness and disadvantages of using questionnaires and/or interviews in the context of your own research.

Such a discussion should appear in your submitted work, so it is as well to begin rehearsing the arguments 'for' and 'against' in your research journal.

Future research questions

Much research generates further questions for future investigation. This takes us back to the students' discussion in Chapter 1 where one student concluded that there were 'more questions than answers'. It is the case that research often guarantees new questions and it is important to state these in a concluding section of your study. Such questions can be alerted in various ways – as a general statement about what is needed next in the field of enquiry or as specific questions of areas of concern. For example, Raymond (2001: 27) concluded a summary of her research study on 'excellent teaching' by saying that: 'further cross-cultural studies are needed which focus also on biography and teaching strategies'. Whereas Al Kaddah chose, in the conclusion of her report, to identify four key areas for future research, stated thus:

Areas for Further Study

In conclusion it is important to say that though the study uncovered many issues which help me to understand the motivation of many of the students I teach it has also, inevitably, identified areas and issues for further research. I conclude this chapter with a summary of four key areas for future research:

- It would be useful to learn more about integrative motivation in connection with the role and status of the English language and how it affects motivation and SLA.
- The research suggests that students' motivations may change over time, but the study focussed on different students at different stages of a course, rather than a longitudinal study of the same students. Much useful insight might therefore be gained from a longitudinal study of student motivation.
- The research did not attempt formally to assess the strength of student motivation but rather accepted the self-report data from students. Further research using different types of observation methods could be beneficial in order to explore the relationship between motivation and success at SLA.
- This study suggests that goals and motivation are strongly linked. There is much scope for research in this area. The students' long term goals were identified in this study but the ability of students to set short term goals needs further research as well as the role of the teacher in setting such goals. (Al Kaddah, 2001: 41)

However expressed, it is important that there is some acknowledgement that a given study has not provided *all* the answers and has played a part in generating new avenues for research. You may not yet be at the point of concluding your study, but bear in mind the importance of raising new questions as well as responding, through your empirical work, to those questions you generate as the basis for the study.

We shall return to the theme of concluding questions in Chapter 8 when we focus on writing the research report.

As you carry out your own work it is possible that further avenues for research may well come to mind. Record these in your research journal – they may well provide the seeds of future research questions.

CHAPTER SUMMARY

In this chapter we have:

Further developed our theme of radical questioning

Reflected on issues already raised earlier about research questions, developing and consolidating this aspect of methodology

Discussed the questioning tools often used to collect data – interviews and questionnaires

Presented some examples of research using interviews and questionnaires

Examined the importance of closing a research report with a statement of further research questions

FURTHER READING

This reading describes a questionnaire survey:

Hannon, P. and Nutbrown, C. (1997) 'Teachers' use of conceptual framework for early literacy education involving parents', *Teacher Development*, 1 (3): 405–20.

These two readings offer suggestions about the questioning and about analysis of interview data:

Shipman, M. (1981) 'Information through asking questions', in M. Shipman (ed.), *The Limitations of Social Research*. London: Longman.

Hull, C. (1985) 'Between the lines: the analysis of interview data as an exact art'. *British Educational Research Journal*, 11 (1): 27–31.

In addition, for a general overview on interviewing and questionnaires see relevant chapters in:

Cohen, L., Manion, L. and Morrison, K. (2000) *Research Methods in Education* (5th edn). London: RoutledgeFalmer.

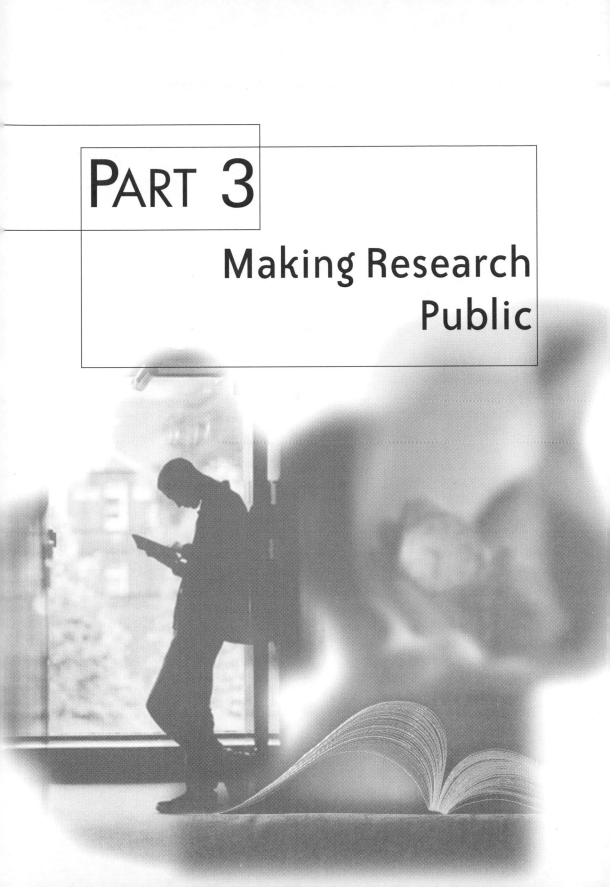

PART 3

Making Research
Public

7

Research Design: Shaping the Study

CHAPTER CONTENTS

LEARNING OBJECTIVES

By studying and doing the activities in this chapter you will:

◇ have an understanding of how research questions can be designed and how their design influences the shape of a study
◇ develop an awareness of the place of radical looking, radical listening, radical reading and radical questioning in the research planning process
◇ have an understanding of a strategy for developing and critiquing research plans
◇ be aware of the critical relationship between research questions, research plans and the justification of research decisions
◇ be aware of how research design influences the interpretation of research data.

Introduction

In this chapter we bring together work covered in Part II of the book. Our starting point is the series of 'radical' actions' which we have already discussed. Here we shall see how *radical looking*, *radical listening*, *radical reading* and *radical questioning* can underpin and inform research design and planning, and how they can be used to critique new research plans. We shall first review the four statements of radical action, second suggest ways of designing research questions and third, introduce a *research planning audit* as a tool for developing and critiquing research plans. Next we examine the critical relationships in methodology between research questions, research design and planning and field questions. We conclude the chapter with an example of a study which operated at several layers of policy development and implementation.

Designing questions

There are many ways in which research questions are constructed. We showed (in Chapter 2) how our students refined some questions for the Crowsfoot study and (in Chapter 5) how these were used to plan the literature search and focus the literature review. With our focus now on research design we want to demonstrate the vital relationship of the research question (or questions) to the research design. Figure 7.1 shows how research questions in the social sciences can be plotted along two axes: *general–specific* and *breadth–depth*.

We have indicated the 'type' of some of the studies at the extreme points in cells 1, 3 and 4 in Figure 7.1. The scattered xs indicate that a study could fall anywhere in much of this framework. There will be nothing at the extreme point in cell 2 because it is not realistically possible to carry out a study which covers everything in great depth and with a large enough focus to allow generalisability.

Activity 7.1

With your own study in mind – try to position your enquiry in the diagram in Figure 7.1.

Use this to identify the main features of the study.

Will your enquiry include a large enough sample to be generalisable (in which case you will have made the decision to sacrifice some depth of detail)? Or will your study focus on a single individual (so giving you great depth into this one case but forgoing the potential for generalisation)?

Of course, your study may well be plotted at a different point in cells 1, 3 or 4 – not all studies take place in the extreme parameters!

Some studies can be designed to achieve *breadth and generalisability* featuring a large sample and a broad coverage of the chosen topic, whilst at the same time

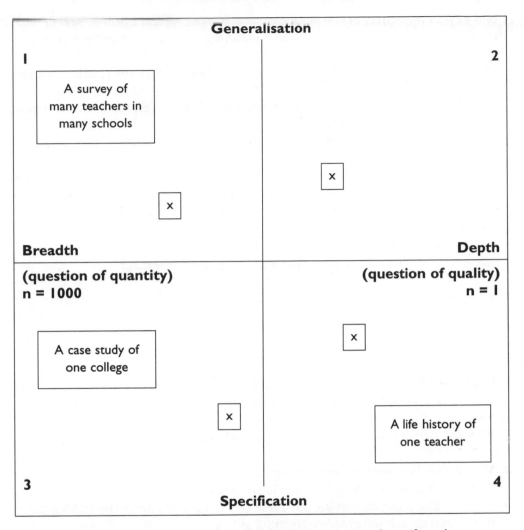

Figure 7.1   Research questions can be plotted along two axes: general–specific and breadth–depth

including an element of *depth and specification* by focusing in on a small number of the participants to follow up in greater detail. Thus a study which examines educational policy can involve many teachers in many schools but could also include a small number of life historical studies of teachers in those schools – we will provide an example of this in the final section of this chapter.

'Being radical' in research planning

Throughout this book we have been arguing and demonstrating the need for 'radical enquiry' throughout research processes. In this section we wish further to develop your awareness of the place of *radical looking, radical listening, radical reading* and *radical questioning* in the research planning process. We have said that:

Radical looking is the means by which research process makes the familiar strange, and gaps in knowledge are revealed.

Radical listening – as opposed to merely hearing – is the interpretative and critical means through which 'voice' is noticed.

Radical reading provides the justification for the critical adoption or rejection of existing knowledge and practices.

Radical questioning reveals not only gaps in knowledge but why and how answers might be morally and politically necessitated in practices and lies at the heart of a thesis, bringing together the earlier notions of *radically attending* to a topic or situation of events.

Additionally, we have argued (in Chapter 1) that social research is:

    persuasive;
    purposive;
    positional; and
    political.

All social research sets out with specific *purposes* from a particular *position*, and aims to *persuade* readers of the significance of its claims; these claims are always broadly *political*.

We have invited you, in the earlier part of the book, to reflect on these statements:

- Why would you want to carry out a piece of research if you did not in some way want to *persuade* somebody of the value of what you are doing?
- There is little point in carrying out a research project (whatever the scale) if there is no ultimate aim to achieve something as a result.
- Research which did not express a more or less distinct perspective on the world would not be research at all; it would have the status of a telephone directory where data are listed without analysis.
- Research which changes nothing – even if this is 'only' the researcher – is not research at all. And since all social research takes place in policy contexts of one form or another, research itself must therefore be seen as inevitably political.

What we want to demonstrate in this chapter is how our definition of social research as *persuasive, purposive, positional* and *political* together with our four processes of *radical enquiry* are integral to research design and planning and how, if these are held central in the researchers' thinking, they will act as 'prods' for ongoing critique of any research plan *as it is being developed*.

Activity 7.2

You may find it useful at this point to look through any notes you have made about the above ideas. There may be issues and questions you have noted in your research journal which are relevant to the following discussion and to the development of your research plans.

Developing and critiquing research plans

In this section we suggest a process which you might use in order to develop and critique your research plans. The *Research Planning Audit* which is the focus of work in this section is a tool designed to help you devise your research plans and then subject them to some critical reflection. The *Research Planning Audit* suggests that you focus first on your reasons for choosing your research topic, first stating those reasons and then justifying them. The process then moves on to the expression of research questions and their origins in literature, experience or some other source of stimulation. Practical issues such as research location and timetable for completion are also asked alongside the details of research methods to be used to gather data. Research questions are then revisited in the light of practical and ethical considerations and reframed if necessary.

We suggest that you work through Activity 7.3 which has been designed to help you become familiar with this instrument as you think critically about your own research design and planning.

Activity 7.3   The *Research Planning Audit*

Look through the *Research Planning Audit* on the following pages. The version which follows includes (in italicised script) our own notes which provide a rationale for its construction and the specific steps included.

Following this version you will find an example of how one student used the audit to plan her research. We have also included notes by her supervisor in response to her work by way of critique.

A blank version of the *Research Planning Audit* has been included in Appendix I. We suggest that you photocopy these pages and work through them in relation to your own research study.

You may wish to use this as a discussion tool with your own research supervisor or with fellow students. Our students tell us that it is worth taking time over this exercise. It requires a good deal of thought and revision but the impact on the quality of written methodological discussion is testimony to time well spent!

Research Planning Audit

Name....................................   Date....................

What is the topic of my research?	At this stage the topic can be fairly broad. In choosing a topic bear in mind that social research sets out to achieve something. Does your topic enable you to make a difference to something or someone?
Why have I chosen this topic?	**Previous research (the literature)** Have you reviewed the literature sufficiently to know where your chosen topic is positioned within the field? Which particular literature has stimulated your choice of topic? **Professional relevance (my current work)** Are there particular personal/professional or policy contexts which simulate this research? What will your study achieve in this respect? **Other reasons (such as . . .)** Is the study commissioned by funders or an agency/employer paying your course fees? If so clarity about this is important. Do you still need to identify other stimuli and a research/professionally related rationale? Does your reason for choice of topic seem sufficient to sustain you through to completion of the study?
Are my reasons good enough?	**Yes, because . . .** Interrogate your reasons for your above choice. Check that they are good enough reasons to proceed. **No, because . . .** Nothing is perfect. Even if you're satisfied with part of your rationale you may still have to manage elements which are not so good! Be clear about the negative aspects and decide whether the 'pros' outweigh the 'cons'.

What are my research questions?	State your research questions clearly and precisely. Remember the Russian doll principle and the 'Goldilocks' test. Do your research questions stand up? 1. 2. 3. **Are there more?** Be clear about how many research questions you are addressing. Keep control of your study. If there are more than three questions state them as clearly as you can at the outset.
Where do these come from?	**(Literature, practice, other? . . .)** Identify the relationship between your questions and existing work in the field as well as professional stimuli.
Can I justify the research questions? How can I do this?	Draw on your research journal, the literature and your professional/personal contexts to write a strong justification for each of your research questions. If you find it difficult or impossible to justify a question then consider revising or rejecting it.
Where will I do the research?	Practical questions are important. Choose a location where you will be able to respond to your research questions. If you have to make changes due to the setting you choose be clear that you want to change your research in this way. If you are not content to change your research you may need to change your research setting.
Have I negotiated access to the research setting? How? What?	Be clear with everyone involved what access you have negotiated. Ensure that key people know about your work and that you understand the conditions under which access has been granted. If you are carrying out your research within your own professional context ensure that you are clear about any boundaries between research and professional work, the ethics of your role as researcher, and the expectations and understandings of others working within the setting.

When will I do the research? Is my timetable realistic?	Create a timetable – to suit you, your academic study plan and your research participants. Check out your timetable – are your plans achievable?
What methods will I use to investigate the research questions?	At this point – think about the four forms of 'Radical Enquiry' **Radical looking, Radical listening, Radical reading and Radical questioning.** Remember that methods are created for particular research tasks, not simply lifted from a research methods manual and replicated. Your study is unique and your research methods will be moulded to enable you to respond to your research questions.
How can I justify these methods?	This is a crucial question. Research methods are justifiable only in so far as they help you to respond to the research questtions. Do your chosen methods help you to do that? What have other researchers done in the past? How have other similar issues been investigated? Does the literature help your justification? Will your methods enable you to conduct a study which is **persuasive, purposive, positional and political?**
What are the ethical considerations? How will I address these?	This is a further question of justification. As you judge it at this point – can you see any danger of your research doing harm to participants in the study either in the process or in its report? Have you weighed your research plan against various codes of practice for the conduct of ethical research? If you are planning to include the voices of others in your research report – do you have their permission? What guarantees have you given them?
Is there anything I need to rethink?	**The topic? The methods? The timetable? The location?** Pause now and reflect on the issues raised by carrying out this planning audit. What – if anything – do you need to rethink? Are your research questions sufficiently clear? Are they robust? Do they reflect previous research in the field? Are your methods appropriate to the study? Will they enable you to respond to the research questions? Can you fulfil your research plan in the timescale available? Are you planning to locate your study in an appropriate setting? Are you clear about any ethical considerations within your study?

Do I need to revise the research questions? Are they clear? Are they researchable?	In the light of the above reflection – undertake one more review of your research questions. This is an opportunity to check that your research questions are expressed in the clearest possible terms. 1. 2. 3. **(others?)**
Where have I got to in my research?	Review your research journal and your research timetable to create a brief synopsis of progress to date.
What is my first/ next step?	Action. What, in the light of your research questions, your timetable and your progress, do you need to do next.
What help do I need?	You do not have to carry out the whole of your study in solitude. Make a list of those who can help you – including your supervisor – and be sure to contact them when you need them.
Who do I call?	Do you have all the telephone numbers you need? Check that this includes the library and details of how to renew loans remotely.

Research Planning Audit

Name......Maisie Jane Brown..............................   **Date**.......29 November 2000...............

What is the topic of my research?	Crowsfoot Comprehensive school seeks to include children with SEN. Following the recent failure include three pupils in succession, the head teacher asked for a review of the situation with a view to the revision of policy and practice. Initial information suggests that the first focus should be on the staff, their practice and their attitudes.
Why have I chosen this topic?	**Previous research (the literature)** Booth, Barton, Allen, Clough **Professional relevance (my current work)** I teach in an 'inclusive' school and try to put policy into practice **Other reasons (such as . . .)** My own child has learning difficulties
Are my reasons good enough?	**Yes, because . . .** The literature, my professional experience and personal feelings come together in this investigation about what makes inclusion work for some children and go wrong for others. **No, because . . .** I feel very personally involved in this – 'my family'/'my child' – so I shall need to remain aware of the impact of that on the way I design the study.

What are my research questions?	**1 To what extent do the attitudes of staff affect the inclusion of children with Learning Difficulties in Crowsfoot School?** **2 What steps might be taken to develop more inclusive attitudes and practices at Crowsfoot?** **Are there more?** Yes – about the individual experiences of staff – but I do not have time in this study to deal with those. Maybe I'll return to that aspect later.
Where do these come from?	**(Literature, practice, other? . . .)** These questions relate to current literature in the field – especially Booth on the Universality of Inclusion (i.e. inclusion is not just about SEN) but also about the relationship of learning difficulties and inclusion (Clough and Corbett 2000) My own work as a teacher is a strong pull here, as is my experience of a mother of a child with learning difficulties. I have several stakes!
Can I justify the research questions? How can I do this?	Yes – because they have been negotiated with the school. I have been careful to check that my own prejudices and experiences are mediated by the thinking of others.
Where will I do the research?	At Crowsfoot
Have I negotiated access to the research setting? How? What?	Yes I am a research student and I have been commissioned to do the study. My supervisor has introduced me to the school and I have met the staff. I have anytime access – without appointment or prior arrangement. I think this means that the head is really serious about the study (and that they trust my supervisor!)

When will I do the research? Is my timetable realistic?	*Initial study January to March 2001 then further work in the following academic year to be negotiated.* *It is very tight but I think it can be done in the three months available.*
What methods will I use to investigate the research questions?	*Interviews and some documentary analysis (SENCO meeting minutes and case histories).* *Some 'radical readings' within the school to pick up a sense of the setting and everyday life there.* *Also Radical listening, looking and questioning.*
How can I justify these methods?	*I've carried out interviews before – though these will need to be very sensitive to attitude and feelings – there will be lots of 'reading' between the words. The only way I can see through these questions is by talking and listening with people.*
What are the ethical considerations? How will I address these?	*Yes – sensitivities about professionalism.* *Also the particular three cases of 'failure' will come up – I shall want to raise them. There are issues about confidentiality and also what I do if I find expressions of really inappropriate practice. I think I really do need to talk this through with my supervisor.*
Is there anything I need to rethink?	**The topic? The methods? The timetable? The location?** *I guess there are – but for now I think I know what I'm doing next.* *The topic is clear.* *The timetable does not offer much leeway.* *I'm committed to Crowsfoot.* *Perhaps I should think some more about the methods?*

Do I need to revise the research questions? Are they clear? Are they researchable?	I've had the benefit of working through these with the group and we've done the Goldilocks test and applied the Russian doll principle. There may be refinements but I think my research questions as already expressed have been subjected to to my scrutiny. I wonder though – should I define which staff? Am I just talking about teachers? Am I including management? What about ancillary staff? This needs a little thought.
Where have I got to in my research?	Negotiated access Got a supervisor Planned a timetable Begun the literature review Beginning to draft interview questions – though I need help with this.
What is my first/next step?	A meeting with my supervisor to talk about what I mean by 'Staff' and the draft interview schedule.
What help do I need?	Help with the interview schedule. Someone to do the cleaning and pick up the children from school on Tuesdays and Thursdays from January to March whilst I'm at Crowsfoot.
Who do I call?	My supervisor. My friend (to ask her to help with the kids)

Critical relationships in methodology

In this section we bring together some critical research relationships: research questions; research design and planning and field questions. In so doing we shall demonstrate how the fundamental research questions influence both the shape of a study and the formulation of field questions. Figure 7.2 illustrates the ways in which these three (research questions; research design and planning and field questions) are connected in any empirical work.

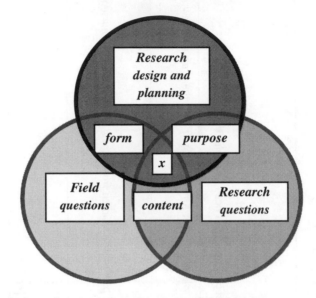

Figure 7.2   *Critical relationships in special science research methodology*

Figure 7.2 shows how *research questions* influence the *design and planning* of the study. Bearing in mind Figure 7.1, the question of *purpose* is fundamental here, for it is clear that the research questions influence the sample size and the breadth of the study. What must the study achieve? is a question to be asked at this intersection. If we examine the relationship between *research questions* and *field questions* we can see that they are connected and that this is a question of *content*. How should the questions be phrased? What shall I ask them? are the key questions at this intersection. Field questions must be phrased so as to respond eventually to the original research questions. Where *field questions* and *research design and planning* coincide it becomes a question of form. How shall I go about this? What scheme, what methods, what words?

Clearly every study will be different, but the understanding of these three relationships as expressed in any specific study will lead critically to the central issues of the study (point x in Figure 7.2). And the issues which lie here are central to the research findings.

Before we leave this discussion it is important to clarify the ways in which *field questions* can be generated from the refined *research questions*. Figure 7.3 shows how field questions can be generated from research questions, and the form and content of these questions will depend upon the design of the study.

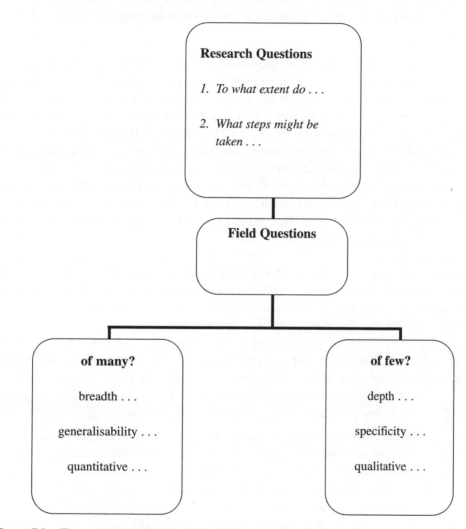

Figure 7.3 *The generation of field questions from research questions and their relation to research design and planning*

In this chapter we have demonstrated the relationships (and mutual dependency) of research relationships. In the next section we provide an example of a research design which takes account of these various relationships.

Design and interpretation: drawing meaning from the questions – an example

Introduction: getting to the point

> Analysis is the act of serially stripping away whatever clothes or disguises an object, so that we can see it in its simplest form.

All analyses – chemical, economic, literary or whatever – share a common feature: the resolution of something complex into its simplest elements for a particular purpose. In this sense, to analyse anything is to strip away from it properties which may be part of the character of something, but which are not essential to the specific task in hand. The aim, then, is to get to the object in its purest form.

This is probably easier for the natural scientist – though some might disagree – who works within a community where notions of objectivity and scientific impartiality are an important part of what defines the community and its work. In such research, though the judgement of scientists is vital, their values and ideology are – as far as possible – set aside, and there is broad consensual agreement about the construction and policing of method.

In social science, however, the situation is radically different, and few social scientists would want to insist that their work is neutral, value-free or uninfected by personal and political ideology. On the contrary, in fact, many would see their work as failing to have meaning apart from its political engagement (see Chapter 1, and our discussion of the 4Ps of social science research).

And so for many, the adoption or construction of method for a particular study is in itself a political act: at its simplest, the way you choose to view an object – your distance from it, 'where you're coming from', the quality of your vision – effectively creates that object. In this sense, *methods make objects*.

> We do not come innocent to a task or a situation of events; rather we wilfully situate those events not merely in the institutional meanings which our profession provides but also, and in the same moment, we constitute them as expressions of our selves. Inevitably, the traces of our own psychic and social history drive us. (Clough, 1995: 138)

Situating a research design

Here we provide an account of a researcher's thinking which led to the design of a large-scale ESRC-funded study. We begin with a brief overview of the study and this is followed by Clough's account of the experiences and decisions which led to the design of the study as it was eventually conducted.

The COSEN study: an overview

Known operationally as COSEN (Construction of Special Educational Needs), this project was funded by the ESRC between October 1989 and September 1991 as 'Teachers' Perspectives on Special Educational Needs Policy and Practice', award no. R000231910.

The main aim of the research was to document the experiences and effects of SEN and educational reform policies as they were expressed through local education authorities and schools, and realised in the daily lives of practitioners. This aim was realised through the following objectives:

The description and evaluation of the structures and experiences of SEN developments within four 11–16 schools in each of four LEAs.

- The exploration in depth of the experiences, attitudes and professional orientations of some 30 staff within these schools, with particular reference to the 1981 and 1988 legislation.
- The relation of teacher conceptions of SEN to policy realisation.
- The development of theoretical and methodological positions within an interactionist analysis of special education.

The schools which participated were identified so as to provide a range of LEAs and of broadly different contexts and systems. There were three overlapping phases of the data collection:

- Interviews with key policy framers in the LEAs and schools in order to build up a picture of the way in which SEN policy had developed and was constructed by those charged with developing and enacting policy.
- A questionnaire for all teachers in all participating schools, seeking information on their knowledge about and views on LEA, school and departmental policies, and about their experiences of those policies in action.
- Life-historical case studies undertaken with individual teachers to explore how their own life experiences, their beliefs, attitudes and values mediated the ways in which they interpret and develop policies.

Source: Clough, 1995: 141–2.

Clough's account of the design processes of COSEN

COSEN started life as some idle hunches about what teachers thought Special Educational Needs were and, in particular, what *caused* them. Long before it became properly a topic for enquiry, I had found myself interested in the sorts of explanations and ascriptions that teachers made around kids with learning difficulties. I'd heard – and still hear – such clichés as 'Of course, he's just like his sister/mum/cousin . . .'; or 'Well, what d'you expect from a family like that?'; or, 'They're all like that on the Elswick Estate . . .'. Even more offensively, and no less current, are observations like: 'She's just plain thick – a complete waste of time trying to do anything with her'; or, 'But why do they come here if they just want to keep to their own way?'

This idea had been coming a long time. I had first noticed it in Croll and Moses' (1985) *One in Five*, where they talk about primary schoolteachers' preferences for different sorts of information about children with difficulties. I had worked as an educational psychologist years before, and saw often in teachers that barely contained need to know what was a child's IQ; not what the child could do, or had done in a previous school, but more: 'what's the raw material we're working with here?' This tendency to a ready causality issues in so many casual staffroom attributions. The drive, so often, is towards reaching to the shelf for so many ready-made, well-worn and superficial 'explanations'.

And I wondered simply where these ideas – about what is 'wrong' with children – came from in the lives of these teachers.

To understand the particular significance of my early wonderings and hunches, it is necessary to know something of the policy contexts of the time. For this was in the mid 1980s at a time when UK public sector education was experiencing integration policies, which sought to 'mainstream' children in – a phrase borrowed from US legislation – the 'least restrictive environment.' And the question that arose from my hunches was about the very ideas of 'Special Educational Need' and 'Learning Difficulty' that mainstream teachers had. In the proposal for funding I wrote:

> The issues and practices of integration make many, often threatening demands on teachers, who may be required to develop new roles and ways of working within new and unpredictable systems . . . Such changes in policy clearly depend for their success to an important degree on the professional orientation and motivation of staff who are charged with realising them. If teachers are seen as mediators of policy in this way, then – both for the evaluation of that policy and for its development – we need to be able to identify and describe the ways in which teachers engage with and feel about their work; we need, that is, to understand what teachers' views are, how they are formed, and what influences they are susceptible to . . .

The *object* of the enquiry, then, becomes mainstream teachers' views of special educational needs. But how do we 'get to' that object? What analysis will help us to
arrive at the 'simplest elements' of those views? What do we need to discard and
what retain?

I realise – much later, of course, and with the sleight of hand of hindsight – that
even my crude, early interest – though apparently inchoate – was in an important
way already analytic. For I had found sufficiently significant – to pin on my wall – a
suggestion made by Wilson and Cowell (1984) in a paper called *How shall we define
handicap?* There is the seed of a method in their call to

> . . . find out what principles and assumptions control the thinking (and hence the
> decisions) of those concerned [with SEN]; and that means interacting with and
> conversing with them, not merely issuing them with questionnaires or seeing
> what they have to say in structured interviews. For . . . the assumptions are often
> hidden; not only from the interviewer but from the person interviewed. Much
> time and effort is required to grasp *the shape and style of a person's deepest
> thoughts.* [Emphasis added]

And another burr had stuck to me: speaking of the relationship between the individual and society, Raymond Williams (1965) talks of the 'fundamental relation
between organism and organisation', and a pointer to method is again evident in his
occupation with one central principle: that of the essential relation, the true interaction, between patterns learned and created in the mind, and patterns communi-
cated and made active in relationships, conventions and institutions . . . [And] we
begin to realise, from experience, that [these] relationships are inherent, and that
each organisation is an embodiment of relationships, the lived and living history of
responses to and from other organisations. Organisation, that is to say, is enacted in
the organism and *to know either fully is to know the other* [emphasis added].

There were others – like the broadly parallel echo in Wright Mills' relation of
'private troubles and public issues' – but in Croll and Moses, in Wilson and Cowell
and in Williams I had a context and a glimpse, if not the tools, of a method which
would provide some answers to my early questions.

What did I do?
My early hunch about how to get to the core of teachers' thinking about SEN was
simply to interview them, in the belief that sufficient purposive questioning would
reveal what I wanted to know about the various aspects of their lives which had
shaped their views and practices. I carried out three such pilot interviews, and it was
from these that I noticed some common elements which were to influence not only
the Field Questions but more radically the design of the study as a whole [see Figure
7.3]. My initial Field Questions helped me to gather information about teachers'
thinking which, even at this early stage, seemed to be grouped analytically around
a number of key constructs. These are represented schematically in
Figure 7.4.

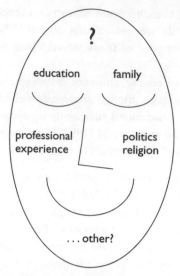

Figure 7.4   *Key constructs for field questions for COSEN pilot*

I have quite deliberately represented this part of the process in this way because I think it helps to reveal both what was 'wrong' with my early thinking, and also how it led to the final design of the study. For one of the things which my Pilot interviews showed strongly was how more and less directly the teachers' thinking could only be fully understood in the context of their workplace experiences; these, in turn, were expressions of given policies at both local and national level. My Research Questions emerged directly from this realisation of how intimately tied up are personal and professional experiences with their political contexts – how, to draw on Raymond Williams again, *organism* and *organisation* share structures such that 'to know either fully is to know the other'. I expressed the COSEN questions thus:

> 1 To what extent are teachers' perspectives on SEN key determinants in realising integration policies?
> 2 What are the major influences on the development of these perspectives?
> 3 How do these perspectives themselves influence policy and practice?

These research questions led to the design of a large study which embraced national, local and school policies as well as personal teacher perspectives. (see Clough, 1997: 141–2) As Figure 7.5 shows, this involved samples of various sizes within each 'level' and a range of methods. The study included life histories of individual teachers (which, if we return to Figure 7.1, we could plot in cell 4) and a questionnaire survey of 984 teachers would lie in the extreme of cell 1 in Figure 7.1.

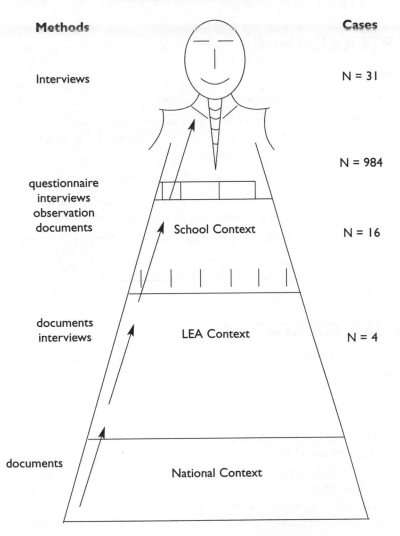

Methods   **Cases**

Interviews   N = 31

questionnaire
interviews   N = 984
observation
documents   School Context   N = 16

documents
interviews   LEA Context   N = 4

documents   National Context

Figure 7.5   *Scheme of contexts and methods of enquiry for COSEN project*

In this chapter we have focused on research planning and design, demonstrating how some of the critical relationships in methodology coincide to create the shape of a study. In so doing we have emphasised the impact of research questions on research design and the importance of critiquing research plans at the outset of an enquiry.

CHAPTER SUMMARY

In this chapter we have:

Discussed the importance of planning research studies

Reviewed the importance of 'being radical' in research planning and the need to remain aware of the skills of radical looking, radical listening, radical reading and radical questioning in the research planning process

Provided an instrument for developing and critiquing your research plans

Reflected upon some critical methodological relationships between research questions, research plans and the justification of research decisions

Provided an example of research design to demonstrate the features discussed in this chapter

📖 FURTHER READING

Rossman, G.B. and Rallis, S.F. (1998) *Learning in the Field: an Introduction to Qualitative Research*. London: Sage.

See particularly chapter 3, 'Planning the research'.

Demn, R. and Brehony, K.J. (1994) 'Why didn't you use a survey to generalise your findings? Methodological issues in a multiple site case study of school governing bodies after the 1988 Education Reform Act' in D. Halpin and B. Troyna (eds), *Researching Education Policy: Ethical and Methodological Issues*. London: Falmer.

8

Reporting Research: Telling the Story

CHAPTER CONTENTS

LEARNING OBJECTIVES

By studying and doing the activities in this chapter you will:

◇ have an understanding of the importance of forms of writing and dissemination in research report.

◇ have evaluated two research reports in terms of their qualities of *persuasion, purpose, position* and the extent to which they are *political*.

◇ have an awareness of the skills and structures you might use in writing your own research report.

Making research 'public'

We argue throughout this book that social research is *persuasive, purposive, positional* and *political*. We also argue (in Chapter 2) that the *arrest of experience*, which is present in all research studies can be characterised by four forms of *radical enquiry*, these being *radical looking, radical listening, radical reading* and *radical questioning*. Through these themes we have demonstrated and discussed the essential methodological constructs of any successful piece of social research. In this chapter we focus on how the above themes might pervade the writing of a research report; how they might be useful in deciding its specific genre and in planning its structure.

'Systematic enquiry – made public'

It was Stenhouse (1975) who wrote that: 'Research . . . is systematic and sustained enquiry, planned and self-critical, which is subjected to public criticism and to empirical tests where these are appropriate.' In other words, research is not complete until it finds a public. In the case of award-bearing courses, research reports may have a limited audience of tutors, examiners and those who peruse the shelves of academic libraries. But, increasingly, students' work is published in academic journals and books, thus widening the audience. In this chapter we want, through demonstration, to continue our argument that the dissemination of research must *persuade*, must be *purposive*, must represent a clearly articulated *position* within the field and that it must have (or seek to have) some *political* impact. We show, too, how in making research public it is necessary also to express the ways in which the four processes of *radical enquiry* (*radical looking, listening, reading* and *questioning*) have shaped the study. Ultimately the research report should not only tell the story but also *justify* the enquiry.

Two examples of research reports

In this section of the book we ask you to read two research reports. Example 1 reports a survey of assessment practices in schools (Nutbrown, 1997). Example 2 is a story which grew out of a larger research study into educational difficulty and constructions of special educational need but which – in its published form – stands alone (Clough, 2001).

We suggest that you first read both examples and then turn to the activity which follows them.

Example I

Purpose and Practice in Early Literacy Assessment

Clarity of purpose is essential to decisions about which types of assessment to use. This chapter takes the issue of purpose and explores the relationship between purpose and practice. Drawing on a detailed survey of 30 schools with nursery or reception classes in one LEA, three themes are addressed:

- assessment for teaching
- the impact of policy
- teachers' assessment needs

The first is given more attention because it lies at the heart of teachers' practice. The remaining two themes are discussed in terms of their impact on assessment for teaching.

A range of assessment procedures is available for teachers to use with young children and teachers have in their hands, the tools available to carry out holistic assessments of early literacy development over a period of time using mainly observation and reflection.

Teachers' reflection on their purposes for assessing are important, so this chapter presents the views of over 30 teachers who, in the early 1990s, were asked to think about their assessment practice, and reflect on the issues which surrounded their assessment of young children's literacy.

30 schools (25%) from one LEA in the UK were chosen to participate in the survey carried out during the period from September 1991 to February 1992, at the dawn of National Curriculum assessment at Key Stage 1. Two criteria were applied:

i.   children age five and under attended the schools
ii. a range of socio-economic areas were represented in the sample.

Sampling was designed so that three distinct groups of schools were targeted to cover the following bands of age range (Figure 1).

Figure 1   Age bands, age ranges, numbers of schools, and proportions in the survey sample

age band	age range	number of schools	proportion of schools in the survey
A	'under fives' only	5	16.5%
B	'fives and over'	5	17%
C	'under fives' and 'fives and over'	20	76.5%

This division of types of school and their age ranges reflected the proportion of these types of schools in the LEA where the survey took place.

A total of 37 teachers were interviewed. At each school the head teacher, or the teacher responsible for language, assessment or the nursery, was interviewed. In seven cases two people offered to be interviewed. All interviews were held with a person with some responsibility for decision making in relation to assessment of literacy. This included: 18 head teachers, 14 nursery teachers, 2 language co-ordinators, 2 deputy head teachers and 1 infant co-ordinator.

The interviews were arranged with the agreement of the head teacher and advisers and officers in the LEA. Each interview followed a similar pattern. In 20 of the

30 schools, examples of record-keeping documentation were also collected. The following questions formed the basis of each interview:

Question 1 *Do you have any records for early literacy development or bits of reading and writing development? If so, can I see them, take copies? If not, how do you keep a record of children's early literacy development – e.g. saving work, tests, teachers notes?*

Look at records together if possible and note how the record works and who contributes and when (how often) it is done.

Do you feel this record serves your purposes?

Question 2 *Do parents contribute to record keeping of early literacy?*

Question 3 *Do children play any part in their own assessment? For example, do they make comments about what they like or can do?*

Question 4 *Is literacy the only subject based record you have or are there similar records for other subjects (for this age group). If so why ... what?*

Question 5 *How do your literacy records fit with National Curriculum and Assessment? Have you developed your current records for literacy since the National Curriculum Assessment?*

Question 6 *What would you say are the main purposes of literacy record keeping and assessment at this time of children's development?*

Question 7 *What would you really like to help you with recording literacy and its assessment? What would really help?*

Question 8 *Is there anything else about literacy, assessment and record keeping which you think is important?*

Main Findings from Survey

Most important here are the teachers' views. The main findings from the survey can be discussed under the following themes:

- assessment for teaching
- the impact of policy
- teachers' assessment needs

In the following discussion the comments of teachers are at the forefront.

Assessment for Teaching

A number of points that related to assessment as part of the practice of teaching were raised. These are discussed here in terms of four broad areas: continuity and progression, parental involvement, record keeping and assessment, and teachers' purposes for assessing and recording.

Continuity and progression

The 25 nursery schools and classes which participated in the study all had record keeping systems specific to the age group of the children they taught. All the nursery classes had record keeping systems which were on the whole separate from those used in the school to which they were attached.

Ten nursery teachers saw records as a way of ensuring continuity of learning experiences between nursery and reception classes.

I hesitate to say passing it on, but it is important. Passing on to other adults working with children so they are aware of what they can do – continuity of learning and experience.

Nursery teacher

... for passing on to other teachers – they're not starting with a blank slate. Not all these 4 year olds will need to learn initial sounds, some know them, learned them at home! So I can tell the reception teacher that.

Nursery teacher

Our new records fit well with programmes of study so they are really useful for transition into school. Teachers in school like to know what they can do.

Nursery teacher

The literacy record goes from reception to 8 years. This next year we will start it in the nursery, but one or two details will need to be added to take account of the literacy development of very young children.

Head teacher 3–8

We have seen children who are really into writing now – I think it will be important to send examples of this through into school so that their teachers can see what they've done so far.

Nursery teacher

There was one case where the separation between nursery and school meant that there was little communication about records:

I've never seen the school records. I've no idea what records other than Achievement folders and Attainment targets they have.

Nursery teacher

The use of Achievement folders which involved saving examples of children's work, teachers' observations, and comments from teachers, children and parents was a way of providing some continuity from nursery to school and eight of the 20 nursery classes had some form of Achievement folder established.

We keep track of writing development through work saving as part of Achievement folders

Head teacher 5–7

Achievement records begin in nursery and continues through school

Nursery teacher

Work saving including quite an amount of written work is part of each child's record file

Head teacher 5–11

Nursery has taken the lead in individual Achievement records, started it off and sustained involvement throughout the school

Nursery teacher

In a small number of cases where individual achievement records was a 'whole school' initiative the nursery had not been involved.

> I don't know why we don't start with Achievement records in the nursery (it runs through the rest of the school)
>
>   Deputy head teacher 3–11

Parental involvement

Nine schools said that they involved parents in recording children's literacy development. In six schools parents of children aged five and over made written comments in children's personal reading note books after listening to them read at home. Teachers also commented in these books, recording their observations of children's reading in school.

> They are useful for informing parents
>
>   Nursery teacher

> For parents to contribute to children's learning and development
>
>   Nursery teacher

> It's for parents – so you can say 'look how she's getting on with this'
>
>   Nursery teacher

> There is a space for parents to comment on the record. They can see it termly, or perhaps just once – it depends
>
>   Nursery teacher

In one case there was a strong feeling that professional trust of the teacher by parents meant that sharing records was neither appropriate nor necessary.

> Parents trust us – they trust the teachers to teach them – it's like me trusting a surgeon if I need an operation. They don't need us to account to them, they see us as the people who have the skills to teach their children and let us do it, it's about trust.
>
>   Head teacher 3–8

A further three schools involved parents of children aged three to five years in commenting on and recording aspects of their children's literacy development, saying things like:

> We have found some ideas for records that staff could use with parents
>
>   Nursery teacher

> I'd like to be able to draw more on what parents say
>
>   Nursery teacher

> We give our record to parents and explain how different bits fit together. We ask parents to fill this in and return to us. Then nursery staff fill in things they've noticed too, then it goes home again – it goes backwards and forwards during their time in nursery.
>
>   Nursery teacher

Record keeping and assessment tools

Not surprisingly, the survey found no examples of teachers of three to five year old children using formal assessment or measurement procedures related to children's literacy. All the work carried out focused on observations, saving examples of children's drawing and early writing, and making written records based on this type of evidence. Teachers seemed content that this was adequate for the age of children they worked with, and some had actively developed different formats for recording development.

i Procedures and processes

Some teachers highlighted the importance of observing and recording in detail, aspects of children's literacy development.

> Two language support teachers developed a record for bi-lingualism ...
> Bilingual records for reading, speaking, listening and writing were developed since the National Curriculum. They are all into observation, record keeping and emergent literacy, but it is having time to share all that adequately
>
> Nursery teacher

> We record separately in reception year because there are so many little steps of development. In the rest of school we record language and literacy on a sequential development ladder using teachers' observations.
>
> Head teacher 5–7

> For literacy there's too much – it's too broad – so saving work gives a more whole approach
>
> Infant co-ordinator 3–11

In one case the school felt that literacy was important, but other pressures had meant that they could only acknowledge that it was important to develop and assess it in the early years.

> It is awful to say but I can only say we're thinking about it. I know that the National Curriculum Attainment targets are inadequate for recording children's literacy development but at the moment we have nothing else.
>
> Deputy head teacher 3–11

This comment perhaps reflected the pressure that new national assessments of 7 year olds caused in the early 1990s. It is a warning that imposed assessment procedures can have the effect of narrowing what is assessed. There lies here, a danger of limiting what is taught and learned.

ii. Philosophy – the need to record literacy

There were varying responses which related to thinking about the importance of recording early literacy development. A very few teachers felt it was not necessary to record any aspects of early literacy.

For the moment we don't record it (literacy development), it's obvious, so we don't really need to write it down.

                                                                    Nursery teacher

Other teachers felt that it was important to record literacy development in detail, particularly because of their teaching and learning methods and strategies.

We have quite a detailed literacy record because if you have reading with story books then you have to keep track of where children are and to inform teaching and learning.

                                                                    Head teacher 5–7

Teaching children for whom English was a second language was a crucial issue for two schools.

80% of the children speak English as a second language. So it is important to record little bits of reading behaviour.

                                                                    Nursery teacher

The record is also a good way to do justice to children's literacy development when English is their second language.

                                                                    Nursery teacher

Keeping a child centred philosophy in teaching, learning and assessing was specifically highlighted by three schools.

We wanted to develop a system which kept children at the centre of assessment and kept process as well as subjects in view.

                                                                    Head teacher 5–7

You have to see what children are learning, then assessment and record keeping is part of that.

                                                                Language co-ordinator 3–8

You need to build on what children can do – work from inside out not outside in.

                                                                    Head teacher 3–7

The importance of ensuring that philosophy was 'in tune' with assessment was alluded to by several schools and mentioned specifically by one head teacher.

Records should match the philosophy. Many things – like tick boxes – don't do that

                                                                    Head teacher 3–7

Another head teacher felt that the assessment of literacy was a fundamental role of education:

I think literacy is fundamental, in our school we would be better thinking about good literacy assessments rather than being burdened with hundreds of Attainment Targets. You can tell from looking at a child's literacy how well they are doing generally.

                                                                    Head teacher 3–11

Teachers' purposes for assessing and recording literacy

Teachers were asked what they felt to be the main purposes of assessing and recording children's literacy development. 18 different purposes for assessing and recording literacy were given and some teachers mentioned several purposes. These fall into two categories Teaching and Policy with six areas within those that were the main focus of comments (see Figure 2).

Figure 2   *Teachers' purposes for assessing and recording early literacy*

Teaching or Policy	Purpose	Specific comments and reasons	No. of responses
Policy	Accountability	• accounting for children's progress	5
		• external pressure of teacher performance and accountability	5
		• legal duty	I
Policy	National Curriculum	• levels of attainment (for 5+)	2
		• track child's development in relation to NC (5+)	6
Teaching	Child's progress	• keeping track of development	18
		• to check progress is OK	4
		• to get a picture of what a child can do	5
		• to record child's skills	I
		• see which reading book they're on	I
Teaching	Diagnostic	• spot difficulties early	I
Teaching	Parents	• for parents to see child's development	2
		• for parents to contribute to learning and development	2
Teaching	Teaching and learning processes	• supporting teaching and learning	8
		• progression (including 'passing on' records)	10
		• continuity	6
		• a planning tool	4
		• to ensure curriculum match for each child	3

The responses show that there are common concerns relating to teaching and other policy issues. These will be discussed later.

Literacy was regarded as important by most nursery teachers. Only three teachers said that for children under five literacy was not relevant. One said that she did not think about purposes of assessment in this area, the other specified what she felt it was inappropriate to assess. Such views reflect the traditional view of literacy held by nursery teachers and reflected in studies by Taylor et al. (1972) and Hannon and James (1990).

It's a bit early to look at literacy in detail, but early skills like matching, one to one, sorting and recognising shapes can be acquired and recorded.

Nursery teacher

Not to pressure them into learning something that is better left until later. We do a lot of emergent literacy – good quality books and lots of writing in play. I have a worry though that we might be doing too much – if we do all this in nursery – what will happen in school? This downward pressure is on us all the time, so we do it in planning and play but it shouldn't be assessed in nursery, it's too much.

Nursery teacher

It's not literacy as such, but the early skills which children develop. We don't have a literacy record, they are too young for that, some of them can't hold a pencil when they begin nursery. So it's a bit early for a literacy record. It would be full of blanks. In nursery it isn't relevant really, so it's not something I would think about.

Nursery teacher

These opinions are in accordance with the views of nursery teachers in a study of nursery education carried out in the early 1970's (Taylor et al. 1972), which found that nursery teachers saw the development of oral language skills as of high importance (p.42) but whilst some nursery teachers saw the development of early mathematical concepts as part of their role (p.88) there was no suggestion that they should play a similar role in terms of early literacy development.

The survey indicated that the majority of nursery teachers held different views of literacy to those expressed by a few of their colleagues. This group spoke of literacy in ways which were in tune with current research and with national policy of the early 1990s, (DES 1990a, DES 1990b).

I'm interested in emergent literacy, we have a lot of children in the early stages of writing . . .

Nursery teacher

With young children it is part of everything, early drawing, talking – so literacy and language is a main focus in nursery education

Nursery head teacher

It's really important to record children's literacy development in the early stages
Deputy head teacher 3–11

I think early literacy development is becoming more and more important

Nursery teacher

We're really into literacy here!

Nursery head teacher

Emergent literacy and early development is so important – we need to do something about it here in the nursery

Deputy head 3–12

Teachers saw three main teaching and learning purposes for assessing literacy;

- to track, map or plot development
- as a diagnostic process which aided curriculum planning and teaching interventions
- for National Curriculum Assessment

i Tracking, mapping and plotting development
The notion of tracking development as it happened seemed popular with nursery teachers. This conveyed a child centred approach to assessment and record-keeping, recording what happened, when it happens, rather than using a checklist to plot pre-determined targets or actively investigating to see if a child has certain knowledge, skills or understanding. Teachers said things like:

so that you know where each child is ...

Nursery teacher

Keeping track of where the child is and relate to National Curriculum

Head teacher 3–8

We keep a check and then can help them along

Nursery teacher

On a single sheet we record skills: pre-reading, pre-maths, like sorting, matching, colours and so on

Nursery teacher

To have a basis of where they are – their reading – with younger children you can see it in their work

Infant co-ordinator 5–11

These comments convey the feeling of *following the child* with some interest, but do not in themselves, suggest a further role for the teacher in extending children's present knowledge. However, this is reflected in the second aim – of assessment to aid teaching and learning.

ii to aid teaching and learning
Some teachers felt that assessment and record keeping was important to the teaching and learning process and should be carried out in order to ensure that the curriculum was matched to children's developmental needs.

In nursery it is to build up a profile of their development and spot any difficulties early

Nursery teacher

To plot development and to plan for the next bit of teaching and experiences the child needs to progress

Nursery head teacher

Literacy is the only subject based record, developed because of a change in reading methods. So that the record is an aid to teaching and learning

Head teacher 5–7

To monitor and support and extend children's literacy development

Head teacher 3–7

Not all believed that assessment and record keeping would aid teaching and learning, but felt that they should reflect on and describe the development of a set of complex behaviours:

We have done a lot of work on early literacy, emergent writing and all that in curriculum, and we do a lot of talking with parents about literacy but we don't have a separate record. I don't feel at this age that we need it. I feel that records should be a summary really – and very brief.

Nursery head teacher

iii National Curriculum Assessment

Teachers made a number of comments about reasons for assessing imposed by the National Curriculum. All schools with children aged five and over recorded Attainment targets on some form of checklist.

In school it's all about Targets now, and making sure everyone is at level 2!

Nursery teacher

National Curriculum Attainment Targets are too broad to inform teaching and learning.

Head teacher 5–7

I don't think the National Curriculum Attainment targets are good enough. There is much more to becoming literate than that – it just shows what is valued, not what steps children need to take. Those Attainment targets don't help teaching and learning, they're just a formality.

Nursery teacher

The Attainment targets for English in the National Curriculum are not helpful in teaching and learning of children's literacy because they are far too broad.

Infant language co-ordinator

We have detailed records for literacy (and maths and science), because the National Curriculum Attainment targets checklists are not enough. We were thinking and working on literacy before the National Curriculum. It is development which is important, so we have fitted the National Curriculum in around how children learn.

Head teacher 3–8

One school had felt a serious effect of the National Curriculum Assessment:

We've changed our minds 6 times in the last 3 years. Whatever we do doesn't seem to work for us. We can't decide on a system which is workable, legal and realistic in terms of what to record and the time it takes to do it. All we can manage, having tried so many times, we've now gone for recording just National Curriculum requirements. Sad really, but what can we do? There is so much to record, we decided to do what is legally needed.

Head teacher 3–11

Some nursery teachers were clear to point out that they did not need to teach or to assess in terms of the National Curriculum.

> We are not bound by the National Curriculum – it's about development in nursery – not targets.
>
> Nursery head teacher

> The National Curriculum does not apply to nursery children – we have not yet bowed to the pressures to assess in terms of National Curriculum
>
> Nursery teacher

Other nursery teachers felt that the National Curriculum had an effect on teaching and assessing in the nursery:

> The National Curriculum has had an influence. I suppose really (on nursery literacy assessment). We've had to develop a record which is useful throughout the school. Attainment targets don't help especially where children speak English as a second language
>
> Nursery teacher

Bi-lingualism was again an assessment issue:

> The National Curriculum does not really take account of the fact that children can be very able and literate in their home language, yet at a different stage in English.
>
> Head teacher 3–7

The comments reveal a sense of concern that the National Curriculum for 5–16 year olds would eventually filter down and pressure in terms of a nursery curriculum designed to prepare children for the National Curriculum at 5 years was feared but resisted. These concerns were realised in September 1995 when the School Curriculum and Assessment Council published draft proposals that became the basis for funding nursery education in January 1996 (DFEE/SCAA 1996). As discussed in chapter 3, further confirmation of downward and political pressure came in September 1996 and again in early 1997, with the publication of Government proposals for national baseline assessment at five years with literacy at the core, (SCAA 1996, SCAA 1997). Such political moves clearly were to influence the shape of nursery education at the start of the 21st Century, with emphasis on particular elements of literacy and numeracy. The implications of this move for early literacy assessment have already been discussed.

The impact of policy

a. Reaction to Government policies

Many teachers' responses were influenced by the impact of recent Government policies on assessment of seven year olds. Fifteen responses were directly concerned with Government policy on assessment. These covered 5 main issues:

    i. restriction of developments
    ii. effects of school inspections
    iii. parents' opinions
    iv. overwhelming paper work and administration
    v. anger.

i. Restriction of developments

The Education Reform Act (1988) has restricted work with parents because policy documents needed to be drawn up and agreed throughout the school. That took time. Also we lost a nursery teacher under LMS so all our flexibility has gone.

Nursery teacher

ii. Effects of school inspections

HMI said that this record is too much – too detailed, so we are thinking again about what to do

Nursery teacher

We think this (way of assessing) does what we want it to do – we're just a bit unsure about whether what we want it to do is 'right' in terms of Government policy and HMI say

Language co-ordinator 5–11

iii. Parents' opinions

The parents think that the testing was wrong – they felt that the children were too young (7 years and SATS)

Head teacher 3–8

So far as SATS are concerned we had a meeting for parents, they felt that the SATs were too time consuming and too much work for teachers to do – unnecessary work load. Parents felt pressure on teachers was unnecessary.

Head teacher 3–11

These views were reflected across the country. *Child Education* in August 1992 commented as follows on the second year of SATS for seven year olds in England and Wales:

... few felt that the SATS had shown them much about children that they did not know already. It seems unlikely the community will learn much from SATS results about the real achievements of individual schools. Research among parents shows that the terminology has proved confusing, and contrary to political opinion, they are not all that keen to see publication of League Tables comparing schools

(*Child Education* 1992)

iv. Overwhelming paper work and administration
Teachers felt that paperwork was interrupting their teaching.

(We want) less paper coming at us
Head teacher 3–7

I think it will settle down eventually. There are still so many changes going on. We're being asked to implement things whilst they are still being developed
Head teacher 3–7

A education in the pressure, a little is good but a lot is counter productive
Head teacher 3–11

Teachers have assessed children for years, but not according to agreed criteria, that is where we undersold ourselves, now we have this imposed and unworkable structure.
Head teacher 3–11

I would like to see the removal of restrictive impositions of assessment, like Attainment targets which are meaningless. The removal of SATs would help
Head teacher 5–7

v. Anger at policies that create pressure

It is right to acknowledge the very real anger that many expressed. Such anger was due to several factors: the restriction of worthwhile experiences for children; pressure of newly imposed school inspections; lack of recognition of parents' stated opinions; and overwhelming paperwork which threatened the quality of classroom practice. Head teachers said:

An end to SATs and a return to proper teaching and learning. Assessment and record keeping is now so overrated, every other word is assessment.
Head teacher 3–8

We were always good record keepers and had good records of children's development in different areas. But since the National Curriculum, we've decided that we will record what the Attainment targets – that is what they (the powers that be) – are interested in. They seem to think that is what is important so that's what we're doing. We don't use our records now, since the National Curriculum.
Head teacher 3–8

Some of the assessment reforms are fine, but the Government seems to be behaving like they invented assessment.
Head teacher 3–12

We feel so angry that they way the National Curriculum was imposed, deskilled teachers, we're all going back to our skills now, now we've tried what was imposed to prove that it doesn't work.
Head teacher 5–7

b. Assessment as a means of accountability

A clear message from the survey was that schools and teachers saw newly imposed Government requirements for assessment as a means of holding them accountable for the progress of children. There was not so much reluctance to be accountable, but a dismay at the criteria by which teachers felt they were being held accountable. There was also a feeling that National Curriculum Assessment was a way of appraising teachers' effectiveness.

> In school now it (assessment and recording) is about levels, how many children have got to which point. It's not really now about children, it's more what teachers are doing.
>
> Head teacher 3–7

> In school there is more pressure, more towards accountability for teachers – teachers feel that unless children have got to level 2, they haven't done their job.
>
> Head teacher 3–11

> In school - now – it is about accounting for progress in terms of National Curriculum. It wasn't, and that wasn't how we felt about it – but now – with things being imposed – we account for children's progress through the National Curriculum.
>
> Head teacher 3–11

> The external purposes of assessment are really about the performance of teachers in the school – not the children. The Attainment targets and SATs are the imposed assessments which are about accountability, not about teaching or children's learning – not really.
>
> Infant language co-ordinator

> For staff in school it is more about accountability now. They worry if children are not reaching level 2 before they do the SAT. Even though they have made really good progress in the 2 years.
>
> Nursery teacher

> On the one hand it is to account for what has been learned – to satisfy the law.
>
> Head teacher 3–8

> Most people keep records now because of the legislation and they need to know where the child is in relation to the National Curriculum.
>
> Head teacher 3–8

The popularity of exploring the 'value-added' by a school to children's achievement gained currency during the 1990s and this trend has shown the teachers' views expressed above to be well founded. The teachers were right. National Curriculum Assessment led to league tables which were used to make judgements about school effectiveness. Assessment of early literacy as contained in proposals for Baseline Assessment (SCAA 1996, SCAA 1997) was in danger of being driven by the desire for 'league tables' of results, rather than an appreciation of children's learning needs.

Teachers' assessment needs

Teachers identified three things that they needed to support their assessment work and to make it more effective:

- time
- in service education and training
- LEA support

Time

From the sample of 30 schools, an overwhelming majority of 26 schools said that they would like more time to carry out appropriate assessments. They expanded upon their statement, giving 12 different reasons for needing more time to work on assessment.

They wanted more time:

- to develop ideas
- to reflect on children's work
- for teachers to discuss children's assessments
- for professional dialogue about assessment practice
- and more help in the classroom
- to think about children
- to read about assessment and record keeping
- to work on our ideas about record keeping with parents
- to observe children – meaningful observation
- to liaise with the next school
- for record keeping and assessment in general
- to write comments on children's work

The following comments indicate how teachers felt they would use any extra time.

Just lots of time to really observe children and add details to records about what they can do – watching them write, or use a book, you can find out so much, so time to make really useful and meaningful observations.

Nursery teacher

Time ... for professional dialogue ... to talk with me as the head, somebody one step removed from the classroom – 'What do you mean by this?', 'What can I do about that?', 'How can I check this?' – real professional dialogue.

Head teacher 5–7

Time ... to really think about what children are doing, where we are going – what this piece of writing shows she has achieved, why I think that piece of writing is good.

Head teacher 3–8

The need for time was therefore rooted in a professional desire to assess children effectively – observing, reflecting, discussing with colleagues, reading and considering next steps. Lack of time can limit the quality of assessments of children. One teacher was critical of her own practice:

This record is not satisfactory to us – but it is what we can do under time constraints.

Nursery teacher

In Service Education and Training (INSET)

In addition to their comments about time, a number expressed the need for and usefulness of in-service education and training on assessment and related issues. Their comments highlighted their need for more professional development opportunities around assessment and the effects that such experiences can have on the assessment of the young children they teach.

i The need for INSET

Nursery teachers identified their own need for specific INSET in the literacy development of 3–5 year old children.

> *I wish we had more courses for nursery teachers – they were so good*
>
> Nursery teacher

> *We need someone ... to lead a day on assessment – to steer it along – a whole day to set us off*
>
> Nursery teacher

> *I just wish we could have some more courses on literacy development . We could do more on records of literacy too – more detail.*
>
> Nursery teacher

ii.   The effect of INSET

Where there had been opportunities for INSET, there was some evidence of its usefulness in developing practice. Teachers commented on the impact of their own new learning on children's enhanced achievements:

> *We've really got going with it – you can see the children filling in forms, writing little orders – it looks like writing too – it's just like ... on that course.*
>
> Nursery teacher

> *One of the nursery nurses devised a record after attending an in service post qualification course*
>
> Nursery teacher

> *Once on a course about assessment the course leader said to me – 'before you do it – think about what it is for – what it should do'. I often think about that – I think we know what our records are for and what they should do. I often think about what she said. At the time I wanted her to tell me what to do, but it was better really telling me to decide what I wanted.*
>
> Nursery teacher

The impact of higher degree courses is evident in the following comment. However, the withdrawal of funding and secondment opportunities for teachers to further their professional development has severely restricted this way of developing and influencing practice.

I did all of this record in my own time as part of my M.Ed. study. Then we used staff meetings to discuss it.

Nursery teacher

As the 1990s progressed much of the time available for professional development in the UK was taken up with courses that 'trained' teachers how to fill in particular forms and how to administer particular assessments and how to navigate their way through particular documentation to fulfil statutory requirements. In the latter half of the decade many LEAs attempted to provide a more balanced inservice programme but teachers' opportunities to attend such courses were limited by school budgets and professional development had been eroded. National constraints and imposed initiatives had the effect of, as Hannon expressed it: *'bypassing teachers' thinking'* (Hannon 1997). Little room was left it seemed for teachers to *think* about their work as their time and energies were directed towards *implementing* externally devised plans.

c. LEA support

In addition to the need for INSET, the role of the LEA in providing support and implementing initiatives drew comment from fifteen teachers

We use the LEA record on literacy development . . . I'll look at the new LEA records too . . . I've got ideas now, with the new LEA under fives record.

Nursery teacher

We are about to start using the LEA record pack issued to schools. I shall find that very helpful in implementing a new recording system.

Nursery teachers

The new LEA record is so detailed – I've no time to do that

Nursery teacher

The Literacy Group has been good for developing ideas on literacy

Nursery teacher

The new LEA pack is unwieldy – there is too much blank space to write in

Nursery teacher

We're really into literacy and it's all those courses and talking about it. We used parts of the LEA pack too. It's quite a new area in the nursery, the idea of early reading and writing. I'm quite new to it all but enthusiasm of other people is infectious especially when people are always talking about it!

Nursery teacher

In my school I need LEA support, publications and discussion

Nursery head teacher

Teachers evaluated the usefulness of LEA materials for themsleves and were able to use these as springboards for specifically developed materials in their own schools.

Record Keeping and Assessment Documentation

Another source of data gathered during the survey was samples of the schools' record keeping documentation. 20 of the 30 schools offered copies of their current documentation. Of the 20 sets of documentation collected from the 30 schools in the sample, 16 had record keeping documentation with a clear literacy focus, 18 favoured a checklist format, 10 used forms of observation and (not surprisingly) none used testing as a means of assessing children's early literacy development. Observation notes and observation according to checklists of developmental criteria were primary modes of early literacy assessment in the early 1990s.

The survey of teachers' purposes and practices in literacy assessment in one LEA indicates that there was, amongst teachers in the early 1990s, strong agreement on the need to assess early literacy development, and a deep preofessional concern that it should enhance their teaching and children's learning. Also clear was that teachers have a range of assessment practice and procedures available to them. Their comments also indicated their percieved need for effective measures with which to challenge adverse and unrepresentative media and Government reports on children's abilities in this field. Two nursery teachers' comments about the usefulness of research:

I think observing children is important for recording and assessing. Observations are also useful in terms of research – there is a place for more research into literacy in the nursery.

Nursery teacher

It's good to hear about research backing up what we believe.

Nursery teacher

What is clear is that teachers in the early 1990s did not use formal measures of literacy and one strong reason for this is likely to be that the suitability of existing measures is in doubt. The search for ways of measuring children's reading and writing abilities at seven years, as required in the National Curriculum, has resulted in numerous changes where no-one is satisfied. Teachers felt dissatisfied with the tests, administration and criteria and politicians did not have the benchmarks they hoped the introduction of the National Curriculum and assessment arrangements would give them, but nevertheless used what they had. After huge public expenditure and hurried trials and development phases an imposed compromise was the result in 1992.

The survey of practice and purpose presented in this chapter showed that an overwhelming need of teachers was time. Given the emphasis on time needed for teachers to complete the proposed baseline assessment (SCAA 1997) there is every reason to suppose that teachers' concerns about time for assessment remain. It is clear that teachers and current practice are catered for in terms of assessment procedures and record keeping processes. However, to carry out assessment with proper respect for children and their learning which diagnoses learning needs and identifies areas for teaching plans teachers will always need adequate time for assessment.

Source: Nutbrown, 1997: 79–99.

Example 2

A version of the following story has been published in *Auto/Biography* – a well-known journal in the social sciences.

Bev: an embodied theory of schooling?

Peter Clough

Listen to this. It's a sort of poem:

> There is mess everywhere. Because he has tried to reach the bathroom there is mess in a trail across the carpet and – though she does not find this for several days – there is mess on a pile of folded curtains by the top of the stairs
>
> There is a way of dealing with this mess; one thing is not to rub it into the carpet, but to pull what can be pulled with a cloth onto damp paper tissue and then to tamp towels hard down, pressing hard down as on dough. This takes ten or twelve minutes.
>
> Matthew is wedged on the toilet; his shoulder is fallen hard against the wall so that his bottom is wedged in the ring of the toilet seat. When Bev finishes the floor he is sleeping and he starts slightly as she touches his arm. She lifts him and puts his arm around her shoulder. There is nothing in the toilet bowl.
>
> In her bed she arranges his bald head cradled in her armpit and when he turns slightly some minutes later his mouth takes her nipple through her nightdress.
>
> It is 4.30 and there is no sound outside. At 5.10 a car can be heard some streets away and some minutes later the first bird starts. At 6.20 Bev turns off the alarm clock before it can start to ring.

Not that many years ago I watched a woman fall apart in a school. The school was falling apart, too, and I knew – without being able to name it at the time – that there was some connection between these disintegrations. The school recovered.

I was working as a researcher, and I'd been studying how schools dealt with kids with learning difficulties. Someone said: 'Oh, you should go to Whatsitsname Comprehensive, that's *very* interesting . . .'

I 'phoned the Headteacher and was there within two days. It was clear I was welcome: yes, they would be happy for me to visit the school; and I could talk to as many of the staff as I wished, and in return I should do a 'sketch' for them.

It's timely. It will do us some good, said the Head. You can hold a mirror up to us. We run a good ship but it will do us good to see ourselves more clearly. We're in something of a Cretacean period *(whatever that meant).*

I didn't like him. He was young for the job – forty, forty-three, maybe – and had a clearly expensive suit. He was tall and bald and his body was obviously trained firm beneath his shirt without jacket. At the time I thought that men like this should not be Headteachers of schools in Labour-controlled authorities. Waiting also in his office was Bev. Bev weighed – when I met her – some twenty-two stones, and was maybe five-feet-six. I learned as a fact later – though I could sense at the time – that she smoked forty cigarettes a day (which is quite an achievement on a full timetable); and certainly in all the time I knew her she seemed short of a decent breath.

She walked [it seemed] always with some difficulty – as if she suffered some continual agony – something which was apart from the weight-given gait.

- Bev will show you round – the Head said – Bev is my right-hand man, aren't you darling?
- There you go – all talk no action. What about my extra .5 teacher, then?
- Bev and I go back a long way, don't we? We've had some fights . . .
- We have that . . .
- . . . but we come out of them, don't we darling?
- When I come round to your point of view we do!
- Don't believe her – it's Bev runs this show; I'm just a suit in Committee

I was embarrassed for – as on a stage in front of me – they were quite clearly nibbling and nipping at each other beneath the banter, the banter oddly freighted with a sexuality. They contrasted so much, Giles spare and tall and somehow his very baldness was vigorous; Bev quite round and flushed and looking hard for breath. And he was at once her son, her lover and her boss; and Bev, too, played.

I couldn't name this sexuality at the time; I didn't know the name of my embarrassment until – in fact – I had written 'There is mess everywhere . . .'

Bev took me to the staff coffee-room and then to a small room off it, set aside for smokers. We smoked together.

- He's alright is Giles, I can handle Giles. We've had our ding-dongs but we know where we stand. He's given me a lot of head – he's given me a lot of stick, too – but we're alright. But that's Giles – if you show him what you can do he's behind you all the way.

We smoked again – cigarettes end-on – and I learned the first somethings of her life: she was single, fifty-one; she was Irish, she was diabetic, she lived with her Dad. This was a list – a sort of summary – which gave up no hint of difficulty. Later I would understand something of what held this list together.

I talked about my study.

- Well in some ways you couldn't have come at a better time; we're sort of in crisis – did Giles tell you? – well not crisis but – how shall I say? – in a melting pot. Giles's a pain but I love him – he's thrown up this plan where we re-make my department – he does this, I think, when he's bored; like, throws in a little grenade just to see what will happen. He's a rascal, he's infuriating but he's generally right, the rat.

I talked with Bev for an hour that day, and again two days later. She gave me a history of the department, and it was then she started to tell me how this history was involved with her own. *My dad became really sick that year and I had to take some time off.* But she did not speak further of him on this occasion, nor actually ever properly. This life and its sadness she hardly spoke of, as though I knew it all and so in the end, by another route, I did.

When we met the third time we talked for nearly two hours of Bev's life as a child in Dublin, a student in Liverpool; as houseparent in a Remand Centre, teaching in Africa, then social work here and there, and finally teaching here. And on this occasion, I remember a moment when she took her cigarette to her mouth, and as rapidly pulled her hand away again, and said: *I really stink.* I laughed and she said I was *up half the night, Dad's incontinent now.* And from this time I think I started to feel Matthew – the dying Matthew – watching.

Elsewhere – out of the immediate compass of Bev's life, that is – elsewhere, things were no better, possibly worse. In the fourth and last week of my visits, I was met by the School Secretary who said that Giles, the Head, would see me at 10.30. It was clear that this was not an invitation as such. He had a simple point to make, which you can hear being driven home in the tape-recording of our brief conversation. It goes something like:

– Bev is poorly
– Oh? Er . . .
– Bev is sick; very, very sick
– I know that she . . .
– and has been for a long time, for some long time actually
– I know her Dad's ill, I . . .
– but short of actually forbidding her to come to work there's not much I can do well that's not true I did I did forbid her one week because she's no use to anyone – to anyone – in this state.

Giles asked me for my report, the 'sketch' I had promised.

– It'll take a week or two to polish, but . . .
– Yes, but the gist. What d'you think of us? Of Bev's Department?

What did I think of Bev's Department? It was in chaos. It was falling apart and was become friable as its Head of Department. Few structures held the thing together, beyond those which organised Bev's own spirit. To be sure, there were timetables, a policy of sorts, schedules for staff to refer children for help. But these things were contingent, mere stuff that routed Bev's energy. My hunch was that when Bev was vigorous, the whole show thrived, was large with her presence and verve. But when Bev began to fall apart – as her dying Dad suffered on and on – the Department, too, sagged. So: lessons were missed, or started late; departmental meetings were cancelled without warning; vital case-conferences were ill-prepared. These were the things to point to later in the account when the infection of the Department needed a name in a report. But what really happened was a matter in the nerves.

For Bev sat the while holding court among the dozen or so smokers who had been granted a separate staffroom. A 15-minute break mid-morning is just long enough for two, sometimes three cigarettes end-on if you leave your lesson sharp enough on the bell, and will always be a few minutes late for the class at 11. If you really have to see Bev you must find her in this smoky room.

And I had met Ken, the 2nd in the Department, whom I knew had adored Bev; who indeed had come to the school just so as to work with Bev; but whose love is exhausted.

- I couldn't *start* to tell you, Ken said. I couldn't *start*/this for starters and he held up a file pinched at the corner between his thumb and forefinger,
- this is a . . . a child . . . a . . . some *scrap* waiting desperately but *desperately* for a Statement so he can have a Support Assistant, yeh? and where's the file and where's it been for the last five – five – months? *I'll* tell you where it's been for five months: under Bev's fat arse in the Smoker's!

And – indeed – it seemed it had been under the crocheted red cushion of Bev's arm-chair. Ken's hair is sticking with sweat close to his head and his shirt is very wet around the armpits. Actually he is very close to tears. From the way he is holding the file you could think that it was soiled.

And every time we walked from Smokers' to classroom, children quite swarmed about her.

- Eh Miss! Miss, me Dad's out on Friday
- Miss! Miss! Look at me trainers!
- Miss will yer tell'im? Will yer miss? I aren't goin' to no bloody doctor
- Miss

But I had also seen her moving like a mayoress or a ship down the corridors, dealing out a word of warmth or counsel here, a cuff or a warning finger there. For all the world like some benign potentate entering court fat with bounty and swarmed with plaintiffs. And I once saw her lead a boy – a young man, some six or eight inches bigger than her – I saw her lead this youth squealing by his ear the length of a corridor. We were passing him bent in menace over another boy – 'bring it tomorrow Paki or tha' dees . . .' – and she led him squealing to her office.

- Ah! Gerroff! Bloody gerroff! Tha'rt bloody 'urtin' me!
- I'll hurt yer, Derek Turner
- Ah'll 'ave police on thee, whalearse, our kid'll pop thee! Ow! gerroff!

Once in her office, safe from other eyes, the boy's curses became tears, and Bev held him on her bosom.

- Yer a great daft thing, Derek Turner, what are you?
- Gret . . . [sob] . . . daft . . . [sob] . . . thing, miss

So . . . the gist, Giles? The gist is a larger than life, smaller than data woman who made magic and chaos around her; loved children, lost files; breathed smiles into hopeless scraps; knew it was hopeless to try to teach Susan Elsworth to read just yet, so taught her to sew; sat on Ahmed Birham's doorstep until his father opened the door nearly five February hours later and just had to let her in; forgot to attend two tribunals, and brought the wrong notes to a third; neglected her body – abused it with excess of nicotine and sweet foods and sometimes alcohol and starved it of the routine health checks and daily blood tests and injections it needed to maintain some sort of exis-tence. She ignored her own illness in the witness of her father's – doing just enough to keep going for another day – and another – and another – and another. What, Giles? This is sentimental? If it is, Giles, so be it.

Of course I didn't give Giles a report. I didn't need to, and he knew I wouldn't. And I only heard what happened to Bev some fifteen months later, when I met one of the teachers on holiday in Filey. Bev's Dad had died six weeks after I'd finished at the school. Bev had sold the house where they'd lived and moved to a modern flat – a-nice-neat-fresh-smelling-flat-for-one. Things at school had not improved, though Bev had by now exhausted the patience – the love, possibly – of everyone but the kids, who still mobbed her. Then a preliminary report by Government Inspectors found Special Needs wanting, and Giles got his licence to act as he had always wanted. He sent for her and suggested some leave; she refused, but he told her to go home and take a couple of weeks, really get over her father. Giles, I was told, 'explained' his long held concern for Bev at the next routine staff meeting. How he had worried about her health for some time – how he had insisted that she take time to recuperate.

I did not need to be at the meeting to know what happened. I had spent a month in the school; I knew Giles, the staff and their confusion of respect and disgust for Bev.

Neither was I there the day Bev left, of course, but I was told of how the bloated and gasping Bev was taken home that day; sent home, actually, by taxi, though Giles would have had an arm around her as she left by the back. And I have an image of her leaving Giles' office all puffed up with tears, all florid and a tiny forbearing smile slightly softening the rictus of her terror.

It is of course a fantastic indictment of us all that Bev's body – Bev's severely reduced body; Bev now livid and finally rigorous – was not found until eleven days after this day. Her new neighbours didn't know her, she bought milk from the supermarket, had no routine callers. Oddly, she was discovered by a burglar who decently called the police (though – for she pungently had no further need of it – relieved Bev of her purse as his fee). It seems that in her anxiety she had forgotten to eat, or else had not eaten prop-erly. Also she had fallen – a gash to her head had bled on to the carpet. Her ulcerous legs had borne the brunt of her illness. There could only be an open verdict. But – the teacher told me – there was enough cat food out for ten days, maybe two weeks.

I don't know what the real conclusion to this story is, for it's not a story simply exhausted by Bev's death. But with the passage of time the story has assembled itself from a clutch of data and – nude of any critical clothes – is simple enough. What is left when the data – the given – are returned to their owners is something simple and terrible; something grave and constant in human suffering. And schooling, it seems to me, is all but theorised by Bev's body.

Source: Clough, (2002: 65–70) This story was published in *Auto/Biography* in November 2001. It is reproduced here with permission.

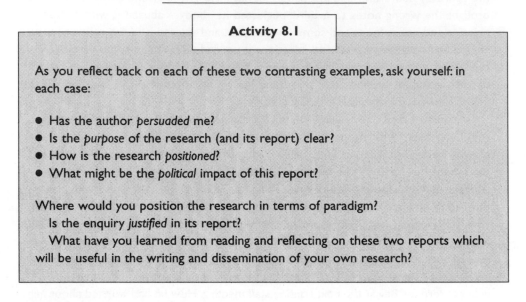

Activity 8.1

As you reflect back on each of these two contrasting examples, ask yourself: in each case:

● Has the author *persuaded* me?
● Is the *purpose* of the research (and its report) clear?
● How is the research *positioned*?
● What might be the *political* impact of this report?

Where would you position the research in terms of paradigm?
   Is the enquiry *justified* in its report?
   What have you learned from reading and reflecting on these two reports which will be useful in the writing and dissemination of your own research?

Reflections

The two examples are very different from each other in style, tone and objective, and they demonstrate diversity of style in research report. So, given this diversity, how does the notion of social research as *persuasive, purposive, positional* and *political* stand up? Is it possible to identify those characteristics within both reports. The following reflections give our perspective on this question in relation to the two examples.

Reflection on Example 1 (Nutbrown, 1997:79–99) This report is intended to *persuade* the reader of the importance of the views of head teachers and teachers on the assessment of young children. Such persuasion is important for the impact of the findings of the survey will depend on the extent to which readers are persuaded by the 'voices' they hear. The *purpose* of the research is clear, to uncover the detail of *why* teachers assess young children and *how* they carry out those assessments. So, the *purpose* of the report itself is to *persuade* readers that this purpose is successfully executed. Without the accompanying literature review it is difficult to establish the researcher's *position* clearly, but the report makes reference to other chapters of the book (from which this chapter is taken) which makes its *position* clear. As for the *political* dimension to this study, it is clearly contributing to the debate which began during the late 1990s about the best means of assessing young children and the purposes to which such assessments were put. (For further exposition of the *positionality* and the *political* frame of the research discussed in Example 1, see Nutbrown, 1997.)

Reflection on Example 2 (Clough, 2001:)   This story is written to *persuade* the reader (among other things) of the connections between personal and professional life – between schools and teachers, of the impact of difficulty in one on the other. Its *purpose*? To report the difficulty of experience, and the suffering of teachers in the under-resourced, under-supported regime of its time – and the common occurrence of Ofsted inspections as the 'final blow'. There is (arguably) no need for further location of this story within the research literature of educational difficulty – the position of the author is made clear through the narrative – though the literature (and the testimony of experience) exist to allow this. Finally, what of its *political* impact? What does this story *do*? Does it provide 'evidence', whatever its form, to support its author's claim that 'What is left . . . is something simple and terrible. And schooling . . . is all but theorised by Bev's body'? (For further discussion of the contexts and motivations for reporting in this way, see Clough, 2002.)

Activity 8.2

You may wish to consolidate your evaluation of our two examples in terms of their demonstration of the four Ps of social science enquiry: *persuasive, purposive, positional* and *political*. The chart in Table 8.1 suggests how such reports can be interrogated to identify these four characteristics and their substantive content. The various cells can be used to add notes about the report. Try this with other examples of research report (or your own writing) using the format in Table 8.2.

Table 8.1   *Analysis of research reports for their four key characteristics of social enquiry*

	Is the report *persuasive?* In what ways?	Is the *purpose* of the research and its report clear?	How has the author demonstrated the *positionality* of the research?	In what way is the report *political?* What might be the the *political* impact of the report?
Example 1 (Nutbrown, 1997:79–99)	Use of 'voices' to appeal to experience	Yes – aiming to find out why and how children are assessed	Clear connections to the literature	Challenging the policy decisions of the time with data drawn from the policy implementers
Example 2 (Clough, 2001:65–70)	Narrative style Appealing to personal	To tell a story? To connect with lives of teachers? To suggest the policy, institution and personal lives?	Indicated through the language used - but no direct reference to other work in the field	Its very existence is a political act. The publication of a story of a teacher's destruction within the colluding system is a political statement.

Table 8.2   *Framework for analysis of research reports for their four key characteristics of social enquiry*

	Is the report *persuasive?* In what ways?	Is the *purpose* of the research and its report clear?	How has the author demonstrated the *positionality* of the research?	In what way is the report *political?* What might be the the *political* impact of the report?
Reference				
Reference				

Strategies for writing your research report

This section addresses the essentials in writing a research report. The focus here is on telling the story of the research. Both of the examples in the previous section are research stories. They are accounts of different styles, but they are both research stories. First you need to ask yourself as you begin to write: *What is the research story I wish to tell?* Having decided this, the next question is: *How can I best construct my research account?*

Writing

Many people write obscurely because they have never taken the trouble to write clearly. This sort of obscurity you find too often . . . even in literary critics. Here it is indeed strange. You would have thought that men who passed their lives in the study of the great masters of literature would be sufficiently sensitive to the beauty of language to write, if not beautifully, at least with perspicuity. Yet you will find in their works sentence after sentence that you must read twice in order to discover the sense. Often you can only guess at it, for the writers have evidentiy not said what they intended.

Another cause of obscurity is that the writer is himself not quite sure of his meaning. He has a vague impression of what he wants to say, but has not, either from lack of mental power or from laziness, exactly formulated it in his mind, and it is natural enough that he should not find a precise expression for a confused idea. This is due largely to the fact that many writers think, not before, but as they write. (*The Summing Up*, William Somerset Maugham, 1938)

We suggest that an important purpose of writing is *thinking*; many of us do indeed *think* as we *write*. We use writing as the tool and process by which we decide what it is – precisely – that we *are* thinking.

Writing is not merely the means by which we record and report our thinking, but a means by which we discover it. It is for this reason that a 'piece' of writing may go through several drafts before it is offered into the public domain. Writing as *process* must not be confused with writing as *product*. The task of committing our ideas to paper forces a permanence of articulation which the spoken word can sometimes evade. But having used writing to uncover our thinking, having placed our ideas into a medium of permanence, it is necessary then to review our words (often with the help of critical friends) so that we can be sure that we have written something which effectively conveys our thinking to our readers, and we must do this before making the report a public object.

Writing for research

Writing is essential for 'viewing' our thinking, for *discovering* what it is we want to say. And reviewing our words and our thoughts once committed for the first time to paper is crucial in research writing. So, here, we aim to consider ways in which students' research writing can be made more effective and, finally, we suggest a means by which students might review their personal research writing strategies in the light of a series of questions generated throughout this book.

Activity 8.3

You may not agree with our suggestion above on the relationship between writing and thinking. Take a moment to consider what we are saying.

Do *you* write to *record* your thoughts or do you, through the writing process, discover what it is you want to say?

It is worth making some notes about this – you may well want to write something about your process of (and purposes for) writing in your dissertation or thesis.

Hannon (2000) suggests that the research writing process might include five stages: prewriting; drafting; revising; editing and sharing. Table 8.3 briefly summarises Hannon's explanations of each of these stages.

Table 8.3   *Five stages of research writing*

Prewriting	Writing begins well before one sets pen to paper (or fingers to keyboard). At the *prewriting* stage writers take the decision to write something and form the intention of achieving some communicative goal.
Drafting	At this stage writers recognise that what they produce can be very rough – the important thing being to get something down on paper. This stage – like all the others in the writing process – involves the *formation of ideas*. Drafting can mean exploring and playing with ways of expressing ideas.
Revising	Writers can move into the stage of *revision* as soon as they have a draft. There are 2 key ideas here: *structure* (having the right structure, sticking to it, and making it apparent to the reader through 'signposts' such as headings, subheadings, and key words) and *brevity* (saying what is needed as succinctly as possible).
Editing	*Editing* is the final presentation of a piece of writing in the form expected (or required) by readers. It requires an understanding of genre and of requirements – this is the point where accuracy of presentation matters.
Sharing	*Sharing* can mean giving it to one or more readers: showing your writing to a friend; submitting a report to one's supervisor; presenting a paper at a conference; or publishing a book. It is the final act necessary for all research writing.

Source: adapted from Hannon, 2000: 98–101.

Students inevitably ask us about the *structure* of a typical thesis or dissertation. We offer the following advice with some ambivalence for three reasons: first, because no dissertation is the same and every dissertation should benefit from original thinking about its structure; second, by the time students have reached the point of writing their thesis or dissertation they have already written, and received feedback on, several pieces of academic writing and, third, the structure of a piece of writing must depend on the research story it tells.

Nevertheless, we are often asked by our students to give them a 'rough' idea (despite having rehearsed with them our objections above) and so Figure 8.1 represents our 'rough guide' to dissertation writing. All dissertations and theses *should* contain the elements listed here, though your own will have its own unique balance which you will, if you are wise, work out in discussion with your supervisor.

We want to suggest something about presentation too. The advances in technology mean that standards of presentation of submitted work can be stunning. We have recently examined Masters dissertations and PhD theses which have included well-produced colour tables and graphics, scanned-in colour photographs, examples of pupils' work, diagrams and other graphic illustration. There is every reason to take time in the final stages of presentation to maximise use of available production facilities to ensure that your final document is compelling to look at as well as interesting to read. Such attention to presentation must add to the research story, but in a way that does not detract from the key themes and discussion.

Dissertation and thesis writing:

'A rough guide' to structure

Title page (succinct and accurate)
Abstract (around 100 words providing a summary of the work)
Contents (lists of chapters, figures and tables)

Chapters
  1 **Introduction**
  2 **Literature review**
  3 **Research context, questions and rationale**
  4 **Research methods and methodological structures**
  5 **Research action** – data collection and analysis
  6 **Research findings** – and their relevance to the wider field of research
  7 **Reflection on the study** – contributions, strengths and weaknesses
  8 **Conclusions** – including future research questions

References (find out the preferred style and ensure that you follow the appropriate conventions)

Appendices (Use appendices with reservation – if it is *really* important ask yourself whether the information you proposed to append should actually appear in the main body of the text.

Figure 8.1   *A 'rough guide' to structure in dissertation and thesis writing*

Caution: The suggested chapters (1–8 in Figure 8.1) will vary from study to study – some will include more than one chapter on, say, 'Research action', others will combine the presentation of analysis, findings and discussion in a series of chapters rather than separate chapters for each element. Studies which report action research investigations might present the report in a series of cycles thus including more than one 'set' of the chapter headings listed above. Some studies – for example those which are biographical or autobiographical in nature – may well adopt quite a different style and structure. Given the potential for variety of structures and styles of study it would be irresponsible to suggest word allocations to the above structure. All students must eventually establish their own particular format in consultation with their academic tutors and drawing on the guidance provided by their own awarding institution.

There are several texts which support the development of academic writing skills and, specifically, the writing of dissertations and theses (see, for example, Crème and Lea, 1997; Brause, 2000; Rudestam and Newton, 2001). Brief reviews of some of these texts are provided in Appendix II.

Activity 8.4 *Critiquing your research writing*

When you are drafting and redrafting your dissertation or thesis use this checklist
of questions to critique your writing. *Ask:*

- Is this report *persuasive?* How does it persuade? Who does it aim to persuade?
- Is this report *purposive?* Does it make its purposes clear? How does it
  accomplish this?
- Is this report an expression of the *positional* nature of the research? In which way?
- Is this research *political?* How does the report connect with and articulate
  political issues?
- Have I justified my enquiry through
  radical looking?
  radical listening?
  radical reading?
  radical questioning?
- Do I need to locate this research within a particular research paradigm?

CHAPTER SUMMARY

In this chapter we have:

Discussed the essential place of writing and dissemination in research

*Invited you to read and critique two examples of research reports, particularly in
terms of the extent to which the authors* persuade *the reader;* achieve some
purpose, *make clear their own research* positions *and have some* political
dimension

Outlined some strategies for writing your research report

📖 FURTHER READING

Hannon (2000) *Reflecting on Literacy in Edcuation*. London: RoutledgeFalmer.
  See particularly chapter 7 'Literacy in professional development'. This
  chapter offers useful advice on writing processes, the work involved in
  getting writing right and the structure of research writing.

Gilbert, N. (ed.) (2001) *Researching Social Life* (2nd edn). London: Sage
  See particularly chapter 21 'Writing about social research'. This chapter
  addresses the end point of research through publication. It discusses:
  truth and persuasion, research literature, reporting research and includes
  clear guidance on the shape of a journal article.

Research Action:
Next Steps

CHAPTER CONTENTS

LEARNING OBJECTIVES

By studying and doing the activities in this chapter you will:

◇ have an overview of your own research journal

◇ have an awareness of the strategies you can use to identify the key sections of your research report

◇ be able to devise your own writing plan

◇ have identified your immediate next steps in your research timetable.

Introduction

This is a brief chapter which aims to encourage you to reflect back on the work you have done throughout the book. In this chapter we suggest ways in which you might:

- reflect back on your research journal;
- identify what you have learned;
- map out the structure of your research report; and
- create an action plan for the completion of your study.

Our purpose, in this final chapter, is to help you move on, to get on with the completion of your study and to make use of all the thinking you have done as you have worked through this book (much of which you will have recorded in your research journal).

To assist in this process we have included – in Appendix II – an annotated bibliography of some recently published books on research methods and methodology.

Reviewing your research journal

If you have used your research journal as we have suggested throughout this book, we estimate that by now you will have written around 5,000 words in response to the activities. Some of this writing will – we expect – find its way into your research report, and in this section we offer a suggestion as to how you might review the entries in your journal and 'filter' them for their particular uses.

We said at the start of the book that a research journal is a personal document. Yours may, by now, be crammed with newspaper cuttings, journal references, odd jottings, quotations from articles you have read, reflections on meetings with your supervisor and other items which seemed to be pertinent to your thinking around your enquiry. Equally, you may have a fairly neat document on your personal computer which contains somewhat similar material. Some of the material in your journal may be there because it struck you as interesting and possibly useful, though you did not know why. In the example we give on ppxi–xii in the preface to the book the significance of Proust is not immediately apparent – but presumably (on 4 April 1998) it struck some kind of chord sufficiently to earn its entry in the research journal.

'Filtering' the research journal is a process which can help to sort the 'wheat from the chaff' – the notes and reflections which are important to *this* study, *this* time can be highlighted. But the rest need not be discarded – in it may well lie the seeds of future research. Here are two ways of 'filtering' your research journal.

Highlighters and 'post-it' notes

Spend some time reading through the entries in your research journal, use highlighter pens or 'post-it' notes to identify entries which you feel are particularly important. Add additional notes to these entries such as 'use in literature review' or 'include in discussion of research questions'. You may wish to number or colour-code these selections so that you can easily turn up all the entries which relate to a particular theme. Your research journal – at the point of writing up your research report – remains a 'live' and ever-evolving document.

Creating a research journal 'index'

Another way of highlighting the key entries is to draw up a new document which acts as an index to your journal – summarising its contents for easy reference. Revisit the activities recorded in your research journal and note where they might be used in your research report. You may find it helpful to include research journal page numbers to make reference back to the original entry easy. Figure 9.1 gives an example of how such an index might be constructed.

Activity	R. J Page no	Focus	Possibly include this in chapter/section on . . .
1.3	6	What is the purpose of your research study?	Introduction Rationale for the study
1.7	8	What difference could your study make?	Rationale for the study
1.5	17	Your research contexts	Introduction – setting the scene
2.5	23	What assumptions do you make?	Justifying methods
2.8	33	Refining research questions	Stating and justifying research questions.

Figure 9.1   *Example of a research journal 'index'*

We have made two suggestions in Figure 9.1 as to how you might 'filter' your research journal; neither is mutually exclusive and these are not the only possibilities. However you choose to 'filter' your research journal, do not be tempted to skip this process. You will have done a lot of work which will be useful to your research report, relocating it by reflecting back on your research journal is important and may well uncover ideas which you might not otherwise recollect.

Deciding on the key sections of your research reports

Reflecting back on the entries in your research journal and 'filtering' the entries will help you to decide on the key sections of your research report. In Chapter 8 we presented (with a number of caveats) a 'rough guide' to structuring a dissertation or thesis (see Figure 8.1). At some point you will need to devise your own structure for your research report. Figure 9.2 offers a way of working out this structure, taking the broad chapters identified in Chapter 8 (Figure 8.1) and providing a template for the sketching of individual research reports. As we said in Chapter 8, this process is individual and the involvement of your academic tutor or supervisor is essential.

Remember, this is a flexible template – not a blueprint. It is a tool to help you develop your own structure as best suits your study.

Title	
Abstract	
Chapter 1 Introduction	*Title*... *Summary contents* *Research journal pages*.........................
Chapter 2 Literature review	*Title*... *Summary contents* *Research journal pages*.........................
Chapter 3 Research context, questions and rationale	*Title*... *Summary contents* *Research journal pages*.........................
Chapter 4 Research methods and methodological structures	*Title*... *Summary contents* *Research journal pages*.........................
Chapter 5 Research action data collection and analysis	*Title*... *Summary contents* *Research journal pages*.........................
Chapter 6 Research findings	*Title*... *Summary contents* *Research journal pages*.........................
Chapter 7 Reflections on the study	*Title*... *Summary contents* *Research journal pages*.........................
Chapter 8 Conclusion	*Title*... *Summary contents* *Research journal pages*.........................
Appendices	*Research journal pages*.........................
References	*Research journal pages*.........................

Figure 9.2   *Structuring your research report*

Getting to it: planning and timetabling your next steps.

Whatever point you are at in your own study, it is important to create a timetable to help you plan the remainder of your study to fit the time available before submission, whether this be six weeks, six months or a year or more. This can be simply done and need not take a great deal of time, but it does act as a way of focusing on the remaining work you need to do and how it might be accomplished in the time available. Figure 9.3 is an extract from one student's PhD timetable during the first year of her PhD study. It simply maps out the tasks to be done into a time frame which allows the work to be fitted into the timetable of the institution where she was carrying out her fieldwork and her other family responsibilities. It does not list the detail of every day, neither does it indicate all times when she will need to meet and discuss progress with her supervisor; it acts as a means for keeping the study on track within the first year of work. The format provides just one example of how a study – its fieldwork, library-based and computer-based tasks – might be accomplished in the time available.

Month/year	Tasks
October '00	Meet supervisor for first time. Discuss preliminary ideas Begin background reading
November '00	Decide on research questions for first phase work and working title. Begin literature search/review
December '00	Decide on pilot field work – series of observations in a single institution. Contact research setting, negotiate access
January '01 –	Pilot study
March '01	Observations three times weekly Interviews with staff Continue literature review
April '01	Write up pilot Leave with supervisor for comment Revise research questions Go on holiday!
May '01	Concentrate on literature review to help refine newly revised research questions.
June '01 – July '01	Devise new interview schedule and pilot new field questions
August '01	More reading. Reflect on the interview questions. Finalise interview schedule.
September '01 – December '01	Move into first phase of the main study Complete observations in the research setting. Complete 10 interviews with staff involved.

Figure 9.3   *Extract from PhD timetable during the first year of the study*

We have provided in this chapter some suggestions for making the best use of your research journal in the development of your research report and of planning your research time to enable you to complete your study in the time frame available. Each chapter has provided suggestions for further reading and the annotated bibliography in Appendix II is designed to help you to find the texts you need for help with particular themes as they relate to your study.

Remember, your study is specific and unique. Your academic tutor or research degree supervisor is a major resource in helping you to 'get it right'.

CHAPTER SUMMARY

In this chapter we have:

Encouraged you to review your research journal by reflecting back on the work you have done in it and 'filtering' it to identify key themes

Suggested how you might decide on the key sections of your research reports and use an 'index' to your journal to help you to structure your research report

Offered suggestions about taking your next steps in your particular research journey

📖 FURTHER READING

Rudestam, K.E. and Newton, R.R. (2001) *Surviving your Dissertation a Comprehensive Guide to Content and Process* (2nd edn). Thousand Oaks: Sage.

Suggestions for completing the dissertation study with topics such as learning style, writing and emotional blocks!

Salmon, P. (1992) *Achieving a PhD: Ten Students' Experience.* Stoke-on-Trent: Trentham Books.

In this book the students and their supervisor discuss their experiences of working for a PhD. Includes discussion of the difficulties of fitting a PhD study with the rest of life as well as practical strategies for the research study.

Appendix I: Research Planning Audit

Name

What is the topic of my research?	
Why have I chosen this topic?	Previous research (the literature)

Professional relevance (my current work)

Other reasons (such as . . .) |

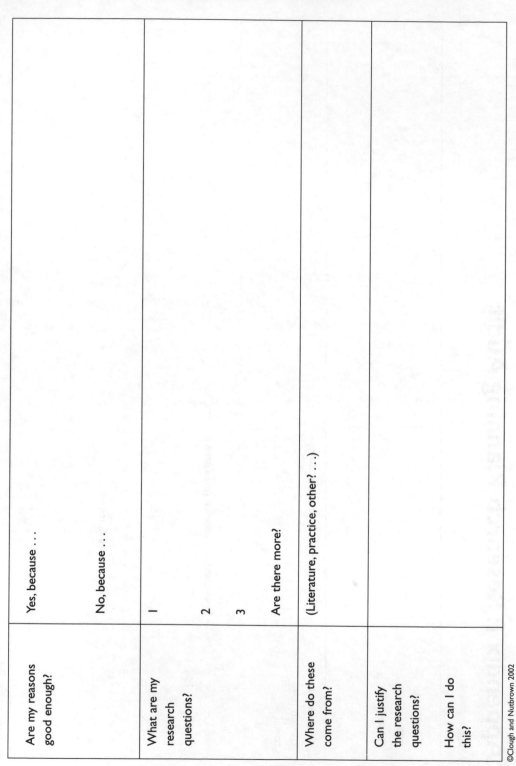

Are my reasons good enough?	Yes, because … No, because …
What are my research questions?	1 2 3 Are there more?
Where do these come from?	(Literature, practice, other? …)
Can I justify the research questions? How can I do this?	

Where will I do the research?				
Have I negotiated access? How?				
When will I do the research? Is my timetable realistic?				
What methods will I use to investigate the research questions?				
How can I justify these methods?				

What are the ethical considerations? How will I address these?		
Is there anything I need to rethink?	The topic? The methods? The timetable? The location?	
Do I need to revise the research questions? Are they clear? Are they researchable?	1 2 3	

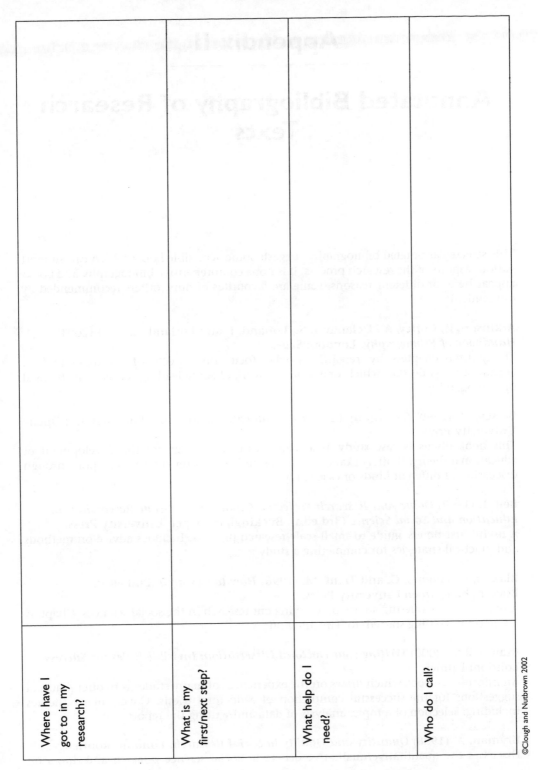

Where have I got to in my research?	What is my first/next step?	What help do I need?	Who do I call?

Appendix II

Annotated Bibliography of Research Texts

This selected annotated bibliography suggests some accessible books which can support various aspects of the research process. It is not a comprehensive bibliography and books appear here for different reasons, some are favourites of ours, others recommended by our students.

Atkinson, P., Coffey, A., Delamont, S., Lofland, J. and Lofland, L. (eds) (2001) *Handbook of Ethnography*. London: Sage.
Thirty-three chapters by researchers who focus on aspects of ethnography. An authoritative collection which draws on the work of some leading scholars in the field of ethnography.

Bassey, M. (1999) *Case Study Research in Educational Settings*. Buckingham: Open University Press.
This book discusses case study as a major research strategy for the development of educational theory. It offers examples of case study development and its report through discussion of different kinds of case study.

Bell, J. (1999) *Doing your Research Project: a Guide for First-time Researchers in Education and Social Science* (3rd edn). Buckingham: Open University Press.
A useful first-timers' guide to small-scale research projects. Includes advice on methods and practical strategies for completing a study.

Blaxter, L., Hughes, C. and Tight, M. (1996) *How to Research* (2nd edn). Buckingham: Open University Press.
A practical book offering advice on carrying out research in the social sciences. Chapters range from 'Getting started' to 'Finishing off'.

Brause. R.S. (2000) *Writing your Doctoral Dissertation: Invisible Rules for Success*. London: Falmer.
An informative book which draws on the experiences of many students to offer practical suggestions for the successful completion of a doctoral thesis. Covers many themes including: selection of a topic, analysis of data and writing the report.

Bryman, A. (1988) *Quantity and Quality in Social Research*. London: Routledge.
Discusses the quantitative/qualitative debate in social science research and draws on

several examples to illustrate these often polarised research paradigms. The book also discusses the combination of qualitative and quantitative research methods.

Carr, W. (1995) *For Education – towards Critical Educational Inquiry*. Buckingham: Open University Press.
A series of papers in educational philosophy which open up the discussion of the aims of educational inquiry and argue that what is needed is an educational science which is not 'on' or 'about' education but 'for' education.

Carr, W. and Kemmis, S. (1986) *Becoming Critical: Education, Knowledge and Action Research*. Brighton: Falmer.
A seminal text which positions reflexive study of education through action research at the centre of the development of knowledge. Uncovers philosophical understandings of education and the democracy of action research in process in education studies.

Christensen, P. and James, A. (eds) (2000) *Research with Children: Perspectives and Practices*. London: Falmer.
A useful sourcebook on methodology of childhood research, this book explores a variety of issues, traditional and innovative – as they relate particularly to research with children. Draws on experience of research in: sociology, anthropology, psychology, history, education, social policy and practice.

Clough, P. (2002) *Narratives and Fictions in Educational Research*. Buckingham: Open University Press.
This book takes a fresh approach to educational research, considering the role and uses of literary and ethnographic approaches. Considers methodological implications, merits, difficulties and uses.

Clough. P. and Barton, B. (eds) (1998) *Articulating with Difficulty: Research Voices in Inclusive Education*. London: Paul Chapman.
This collection addresses the issue of 'voice' in research. Includes consideration of power-relations, emancipatory research, democratic approaches and identity.

Clough, P. and Corbett, J. (2000) *Theories of Inclusive Education: a Students' Guide*. London: Paul Chapman/Sage.
Dealing with the development of theoretical perspectives on inclusive education, this book concludes with examples of students' work and demonstrates how theory can be linked – through small-scale studies – with practice.

Clough. P. and Nutbrown, C. (eds) (2001) *Voices of Arabia: Essays in Educational Research*. Sheffield: University of Sheffield Papers in Education.
In this book nine accounts of Masters' students' work focus on a range of methodological issues often confronted by students carrying out small-scale studies for academic awards.

Cohen, L., Mannion, L. and Morrison, K. (2000) *Research Methods in Education* (5th edn). London: RoutledgeFalmer.
A comprehensive guide to research methods with discussion of methods and theoretical underpinnings of aspects of methodology. Covers research context, research planning, 'styles' of research, strategies for data collection and recent developments such as use of the Internet.

Crème, P. and Lea, M.R. (1997) *Writing at University: a Guide for Students*. Buckingham: Open University Press.
A practical guide which opens up the writing process to offer strategies to support students in developing their academic writing skills.

de Laine, M. (2000) *Fieldwork, Participation and Practice: Ethics and Dilemmas in Qualitative Research*. Thousand Oaks: Sage.
This book examines ethics in fieldwork through examples of fieldwork that confront and deal with ethical problems and dilemmas.

de Vaus, D. (2001) *Research Design in Social Research*. London: Sage.
This book emphasises the structure and design of research and describes the main types of research design in social science research. Strategies for the evaluation of research design are included as well as practical tuition which supports students in the development of design skills.

Denscombe, M. (1998) *The Good Research Guide for Small-scale Social Research Projects*. Buckingham: Open University Press.
This book suggests practical ways in which students can develop and complete successful small-scale studies within a set time-frame.

Denzin, N.K. (1997) *Interpretive Ethnography: Ethnographic Practices for the 21st Century*. London: Sage.
A seminal text on narrative approaches to ethnography. Traces the origins and practices of the ethnographic project and anticipates its future.

Denzin, N.K. and Lincoln, Y.S. (eds) (2000) *Handbook of Qualitative Research* (2nd edn). Thousand Oaks: Sage.
An impressive and important volume that represents theory and practice of qualitative inquiry. Some 20 chapters on topics such as autoethnography, critical race theory, applied ethnography and queer theory.

Denzin, N.K. and Lincoln, Y.S. (eds) (2000) *The Qualitative Inquiry Reader*, London: Sage.
A selection of articles from the journal *Qualitative Inquiry*. There are papers from a range of research disciplines organised in five sections: reflexive ethnography, auto-ethnography, poetics, performance narratives and assessing the text.

Flick, U. (1998) *Introduction to Qualitative Research* (2nd edn). London: Sage.
A student-friendly introductory text on qualitative research. Discusses theories and methods with examples and useful reading lists.

Gilbert, N. (ed.) (2001) *Researching Social Life* (2nd edn). London: Sage.
This book covers many issues, strategies and skills important to social science research including research methods, data gathering techniques, data analysis, computer analysis and critical understanding of policy and theory. Tackles some challenging topics with clarity and practical advice.

Gitlin, A. (ed.) (1994) *Power and Method: Political Activism and Educational Research*. London: Routledge.
In this book a number of leading researchers discuss issues of power in the research process. Examining research from multiple and different perspectives the contributors focus on

political activism in research and challenge the accepted status of traditional assumptions about the importance of such issues as validity, objectivity and research 'subjects'.

Gubrium, J.F. and Holstein, J.A. (eds) (2001) *Handbook of Interview Research Context and Method*. **Thousand Oaks: Sage.**
Examines the interview in contemporary society as the main research method in the social sciences. Both theory and practical advice are thoroughly addressed. Argues that interviews are much more than a method of data gathering, rather they are integral to society.

Halpin, D. and Tropyna, B (1994) *Researching Education Policy: Ethical and Methodological Issues*. **London: Falmer.**
A collection of essays which focus on the ethical and methodological issues arising from some major studies in educational policy.

Hart, C. (1998) *Doing a Literature Review: Releasing the Social Science Research Imagination*. **London: Sage/The Open University.**
Provides advice on the skills and strategies needed in order to write a review of research literature. A practical guide which covers literature review, classification, argument, organisation of ideas and writing the review.

Hart, C. (2001) *Doing a Literature Search: a Comprehensive Guide for the Social Sciences*. **London: Sage/The Open University.**
A comprehensive text which provides practical advice on searching the literature of a research study. Includes coverage of management of the search, types of literature, and using information communications technology.

Holliday, A. (2001) *Doing and Writing Qualitative Research*. **London: Sage.**
Suggests, step by step, how to write-up qualitative research studies. The book includes 20 examples of writing to help students make the necessary decisions to produce a written research report.

Hollway, W. and Jefferson, T. (2000) *Doing Qualitative Research Differently: Free Association, Narrative and the Interview Method*. **London: Sage.**
This book provides a critical review of methods used in qualitative research and offers practical suggestions about how to use them. Examples from research are included to demonstrate the uses of the free-association interview method.

Hopkins, D. (2002) *A Teacher's Guide to Classroom Research* (3rd edn). **Buckingham: Open University Press.**
A practical guide to conducting classroom enquiry focuses on the practical skills and challenges and discusses the professionalisation of schools through practitioner research.

Miles, M.B. and Huberman, A.M. (1994) *Qualitative Data Analysis: an Expanded Sourcebook*. **London: Sage.**
A comprehensive text which details approaches to analysis and interpretation of qualitative data.

Moore, N. (2000) *How to Do Research: the Complete Guide to Designing and Managing Research Projects* (3rd edn). **London: Library Association Publishing.**
A guide for beginning researchers with advice on developing an effective study, the book includes suggestions on research objectives, planning, financial support, research

management, conclusions and recommendations, report writing and dissemination, as well as some discussion of popular research methods.

Nutbrown, C. (ed.) (2002) *Research Studies in Early Childhood Education.* **Stoke-on-Trent: Trentham Books.**
In this book 13 accounts of small-scale studies in early childhood education discuss a range of methodological issues often confronted by students carrying out small-scale studies for academic awards.

Patton, M.Q. (1999) *Qualitative Research and Evaluation Methods* **(3rd edn). Thousand Oaks: Sage.**
This book provides much practical guidance on qualitative design, sampling, interviewing, historical perspectives, ethical issues, fieldwork, observation and qualitative analysis.

Pink, S. (2001) *Doing Visual Ethnography: Images, Media and Representation in Research.* **London: Sage.**
This book explores the potential of photography, video and hypermedia in ethnographic and social research. The research process is illustrated from planning the project to publication.

Pring, R. (2001) *Philosophy of Educational Research.* **London: Continuum.**
An important synthesis of philosophical issues focusing on philosophy of mind, epistemology, philosophy of social science, ethics and the philosophy of education.

Reason, P. and Bradbury, H. (eds) (2001) *Handbook of Action Research: Participative Inquiry and Practice.* **London: Sage.**
Discusses action research in the postmodern context, drawing together different strands of action research and demonstrating their applications.Clear exposition of current approaches to action research in social inquiry.

Rodriguez, N. and Ryave, A. (2002) *Systematic Self-Observation.* **Thousand Oaks: Sage.**
Outlines a method of gathering data on 'hidden' social actions: systematic self-observation (SSO). Provides suggestions on using thoughts, emotions and other less visible actions as data.

Rudduck, J. and McIntyre, D. (eds) (1998) *Challenges for Educational Research.* **London: BERA/Paul Chapman.**
Chapters by 16 major figures in educational research focusing on the future direction of educational research in the twenty-first century.

Rudestam, K.E. and Newton, R.R. (2001) *Surviving your Dissertation: a Comprehensive Guide to Content and Process* **(2nd edn). Thousand Oaks: Sage.**
A useful guide to completing a dissertation or thesis. Includes suggestions on selecting a topic, literature review, data overload, argument, analysis and report.

Salmon, P. (1992) *Achieving a PhD: Ten Students' Experience.* **Stoke-on-Trent: Trentham Books.**
In this book students convey their personal and academic experiences as they completed their PhD studies. Focuses on PhD journeys and their impact on aspects of daily and family life as well as providing solutions to research-oriented problems.

Scheurich, J.J. (1997) *Research Method in the Postmodern.* London: Falmer.
This book presents a postmodern discussion of research methodology with consideration of the critique of research approaches. It describes and demonstrates the implications of postmodernism for research practice.

Schwandt, T.A. (2001) *Dictionary of Qualitative Inquiry* (2nd edn). Thousand Oaks:
Sage.
An accessible guide to terms and phrases used in qualitative inquiry. Not to be seen
simply as a technical guide to qualitative methods, rather a conceptual and theoretical
guide to qualitative studies

Silverman, D. (2000) *Doing Qualitative Research: a Practical Handbook.* London:
Sage.
This book offers students a practical guide to successful completion of a research study.
Methodological issues are discussed and practical solutions to research challenges are
offered.

Silverman, D. (2001) *Interpreting Qualitative Data: Methods for Analysing Talk,
Text and Interaction* (2nd edn). London: Sage.
A clearly written general textbook in qualitative methods which presents recent developments, methodologies, and interpretive strategies in qualitative research Many useful
exercises, summaries of key points and recommended readings.

Taylor, S. (ed.) (2001) *Ethnographic Research: a Reader.* London: Open University
Press/Sage.
A selection of ten recently published studies illustrates the range of ethnographic studies in social research. Guided reading exercises help students to appreciate researchers'
assumptions, positions, methods and theoretical approaches.

Travers, M. (2001) *Qualitative Research through Case Studies.* London: Sage.
This book focuses on aspects of analysis introducing a number of interpretive
approaches. Case studies are used to introduce theoretical assumptions of case study and
various analytical approaches.

Walker, R. (1985) *Doing Research – a Handbook for Teachers.* London: Methuen.
A practical text which discusses issues and strategies in doing practitioner research in
schools.

Warren, C.A.B. and Hackney, J.K. (2000) *Gender Issues in Ethnography* (2nd edn).
London: Sage.
A summary of gender issues in fieldwork, this book demonstrates how the researcher's
gender affects fieldwork relationships, ethnographic study and its report.

Wolcott, H.F. (2001) *Writing Up Qualitative Research* (2nd edn). London: Sage.
A useful book with examples and suggestions for writing up a qualitative study. Provides
advice on producing a report from qualitative data.

References

Al Kaddah, S. (2001) 'Motivation and learning a second language', in P. Clough and C. Nut-brown (eds), *Voices of Arabia: Essays in Educational Research*. Sheffield: University of Sheffield Papers in Education.

Anderson, K., Armitage, S., Jack, D. amd Wittner, J. (1990) 'Beginning where we are: feminist methodology in oral history', in J. McCarl-Nielsen (ed.) *Feminist Research Methods: Exemplary Readings in the Social Sciences*. London: Westview Press.

Anning, A. (1997) *The First Years at School* (2nd edn.) Buckingham: Open University Press.

Barrs, M., Ellis, S., Hester, H. and Thomas, A. (1989) *The Primary Language Record*. London: Inner London Education Authority/Centre for Language in Primary Education.

Barton, L. (ed.) (1996) *Disability and Society: Emerging Issues and Insights*. London: Longman.

Beck, L.C., Trombetta, W.L. and Share, S. (1986) 'Using focus group sessions before decisions are made', *North Carolina Medical Journal*, 47 (2): 73–4.

Berry, T. (2001) 'Does inclusion work? A case study of four children'. Unpublished MA in Early Childhood Education dissertation. Sheffield, University of Sheffield.

Blaxter, L., Hughes, C. and Tight, M. (2001) *How to Research* (2nd edn). Buckingham: Open University Press.

Bolton, N. (1972) *The Psychology of Thinking*. London: Cassell.

Booth, T. (2000) 'Reflection', in P. Clough and J. Corbett *Theories of Inclusive Education: a Students' Guide*. London: Paul Chapman/Sage.

Booth, T., Ainscow, M., Black-Hawkins, K., Vaughan, M. and Shaw, L. (2000) *Index for Inclusion: Developing Learning and Participation in Schools*. Bristol: Centre for Studies in Inclusive Education.

Brause, R.S. (2000) *Writing your Doctoral Dissertation: Invisible Rules for Success*. London: Falmer.

Brimer, A., and Raban, B. (1979) *Administrative Manual for the Infant Reading Tests*. Education Evaluation Enterprises.

Bruce, T. et. al. (1997) *Recurring themes in Early Childhood Education*. London: Paul Chapman.

Bruce, T., Findlay, A., Read, J. and Scarborough, M. (1995) *Recurring Themes in Education*. London: Paul Chapman Publishing.

Byers, P.Y. and Wilcox, J.R. (1988). *Focus Groups: an Alternative Method of Gathering Qualitative Data in Communication Research* (Report No. CS-506–291). New Orleans, LA:

Speech Communication Association. (ERIC Document Reproduction Service No. ED 297 393).

Carr, W. (1995) *For Education – towards Critical Educational Inquiry.* Buckingham: Open University Press.

Clay, M. (1972) *The Early Detection of Reading Difficulties: a diagnostic survey.* Auckland, NZ: Heinemann Education Books.

Clough, P. (1995) 'Problems of identity and method in the investigation of special needs', in P. Clough and L. Barton (eds) *Making Difficulties: Research and the Construction of Special Educational Needs.* London: Paul Chapman.

Clough, P. (1996) ' "Again Fathers and Sons': the mutual construction of self, story and special educational needs', *Disability and Society,* 112, (1): 71–81.

Clough, P. (ed.) (1998a) *Managing Inclusive Education: From Policy to Experience.* London Paul Chapman/Sage.

Clough, P. (1998b) 'Bridging "mainstream" and 'special' education: a curriculum problem', *Curriculum Studies,* 20 (4): 327–38.

Clough, P. (1998c) Differently articulate? Some indices of disturbed/disturbing voices. In P. Clough and L. Barton (eds) (1998) *Articulating with Difficulty: Research Voices in Inclusive Education.* London: Paul Chapman.

Clough, P. (1999) 'Exclusive tendencies: concepts, consciousness and curriculum in the project of inclusion', *International Journal of Inclusive Education,* 3 (1): 63–73.

Clough, P. (2000) 'Routes to inclusion', in P. Clough and J. Corbett *Theories of Inclusive Education.* London: Paul Chapman/Sage.

Clough, P. (2001) 'Bev: an embodied theory of schooling' *Auto/Biography,* 9 (1 and 2): 123–125.

Clough, P. (2002) *Narratives and Fictions in Educational Research* Buckingham: Open University Press.

Clough, P. and Barton, L. (eds) (1995) *Making Difficulties: Research and the Construction of Special Educational Needs.* London: Paul Chapman.

Clough P. and Barton, L. (eds) (1998) *Articulating with Difficulty: Research Voices in Inclusive Education.* London: Paul Chapman.

Clough, P. and Corbett, J. (2000) *Theories of Inclusive Education: a Students' Guide.* London: Paul Chapman/Sage.

Clough, P. and Nutbrown, C. (eds) (2001) *Voices of Arabia: Essays in Educational Research.* Sheffield: University of Sheffield Papers in Education.

Clymer, T. and Barrett, T.C. (1983) *Clymer-Barrett Readiness Test (CBRT).* Chapman, Brook and Kent, USA.

Cohen, L. Manion, L. and Morrison, K. (2000) *Research Methods in Education* (5th edn.) London: RoutledgeFalmer.

Corbett, J. (1996) *'Badmouthing': The Language of Special Needs.* London: Falmer.

Corbett, J. (1998) *Special Educational Needs in the Twentieth Century: a Cultural Analysis.* London: Cassell.

Crème, P. and Lea, M.R. (1997) *Writing at University: a Guide for Students.* Buckingham: Open University Press.

Croll, P. and Moses, D. (1985) *One in Five: The Assessment and Incidence of Special Education Needs.* London: Routledge and Kegan Paul.

de Vaus, D. (2001) *Research Design in Social Research.* London: Sage.

Demn, R. and Brehony, K.J. (1994) 'Why didn't you use a survey to generalise your findings? Methodological issues in a multiple site case study of school governing bodies after the 1988 Education Reform Act', in D. Halpin and B. Troyna (eds), *Researching Education Policy: Ethical and Methodological Issues*. London: Falmer.

Denscombe, M. (1998) *The Good Research Guide for Small-scale Social Research Projects*. Buckingham: Open University Press.

Denzin, N.K. and Lincoln, Y.S. (eds) (2000) *The Handbook of Qualitative Research* (2nd edn). Thousand Oaks: Sage.

Department for Education and Employment (DFEE) (1996) *Education Act 1996*. London: HMSO.

Department of Education and Science (DES) (1981) *Education Act 1981*. London: HMSO.

Department of Education and Science (1988) Education Act 1988. London: HMSO.

Dessent, T. (1983) *Making the Ordinary School Special*. Lewes: Falmer Press.

Downing, J. and Thackray, D. (1976) *Reading Readiness Inventory*. London: Hodder and Stoughton.

Downing, J., Ayres, D.M., and Schaeffer, B. (1983) *Linguistic Awareness in Reading Readiness (LARR)*. London: National Foundation for Educational Research – Nelson.

Edwards P.A. (1989) *Supporting lower SES mothers' attempts to provide scaffolding for book reading*, in J. Allen and J.M. Mason (eds) *Risk Makers, Risk Breakers: reducing the risks for young literacy learners*. Portsmouth: Heinemann.

Fine, M. (1994) 'Dis-stance and other stances: negotiations of power inside feminist research', in A. Gitlin (ed.) *Power and Method: Political activism and educational research*. London: Routledge.

Fontana, A. and Frey, J.H. (2000) 'The interview: from structured questions to negotiated text' in N.K. Denzin and Y.S. Lincoln (eds), *The Handbook of Qualitative Research*. London: Sage.

Foster, P. (1996) *Observing Schools: a Methodological Guide*. London: Paul Chapman.

Gilbert, N. (ed.) (2001) *Researching Social Life* (2nd edn). London: Sage.

Golbv, M. and Gulliver, R.J. (1979) 'Whose remedies, whose ills? A critical review of remedial education', *Journal of Curriculum Studies*, 11: 137–47.

Goldsmith, E. and Handel, R. (1990) *Family Reading: an intergenerational approach to literacy*. Syracuse: New Readers Press.

Goodwin, W.L. and Goodwin, L.D. (1996) *Understanding Quantitative and Qualitative Research in Early Childhood Education*. New York: Teachers College Press.

Green, C. (1987) Parental facilitation of young children's writing *Early Child Development and Care*, 28: 31–37.

Griffiths, A. and Edmonds, M. (1986) *Report on the Calderdale Pre-school Parent Bood Project*. Halifax: Schools Psychological Service, Calderdale Education Department.

Halpin, D. and Tropyna, B. (1994) *Researching Education Policy: Ethical and Methodological Issues*. London: Falmer.

Hannon, P. (1998) 'An ecological perspective on educational research', in J. Rudduck and D. McIntyre (eds), *Challenge for Educational Research*. London: Paul Chapman.

Hannon, P. (2000) *Reflecting on Literacy in Education*. London: RoutledgeFalmer.

Hannon, P. and Nutbrown, C. (1997) *Teachers' Use of a Conceptual Framework for Early Literacy Education Involving Parents. Teacher Development*, (3): 405–420.

Hannon, P. and Nutbrown, C. (2001) *Emerging Findings from an Experimental Study of Early Literacy Education involving Parents*. Paper presented at the United Kingdom Reading Association Annual Conference, Canterbury Christ Church University College.

Hart, C. (1998) *Doing a Literature Review: Releasing the Social Science Research Imagination*. London: Sage/The Open University.

Hart. C. (2001) *Doing a Literature Search: a Comprehensive Guide for the Social Sciences*. London: Sage/The Open University.

Hegel, G.W.F. (1894) *Hegel's Philosophy of Mind* (trans. W. Wallace). Oxford: Clarendon Press.

Herbert, E. (1998) Included from the start? Managing Early Years settings for All, in P. Clough (ed.) (1998) *Managing Inclusive Education: From Policy to Experience*. London: Paul Chapman.

Hess, J.M. (1968). 'Group interviewing', in R. L. King (ed.) *New science of planning*. Chicago: American Marketing Association.

Hull, C. (1985), 'Between the lines: the analysis of interview data as an exact art', *British Educational Research Journal*, 11 (1): 27–31.

Husserl, E. (1901) *Logical Investigations*, vols 1 and 2. Halle: Niemeyer.

Jones, C. (1998) 'A study of teachers' perspectives on the inclusion of pupils with SEN in mainstream schools'. Unpublished MSc study, Division of Education, University of Sheffield.

Jones, M. and Hendrickson, N. (1970) Recognition by preschool children of advertised products and book covers. *Journal of Home Economics*. 62, (4): 263–267.

Khan, R. (2002) 'No need to smack', in C. Nutbrown (ed.) *Research Studies in Early Childhood Education*. Stoke-on-Trent: Trentham Books.

Kaplan, A. (1973) *The Conduct of Inquiry*. Aylesbury: Intertext Books.

Kent LEA (1992) *Reading Assessment Profile*. Kent: Kent County Council.

Kiesinger, C.E. (1998) 'From interviewing to story: writing Abbie's life', *Qualitative Inquiry*, 4 (1): 71–95.

Koch, C. (2001) 'Choosing post-secondary education: what influences women students?', in P. Clough, and C. Nutbrown (eds), *Voices of Arabia: Essays in Educational Research*. Sheffield: University of Sheffield Papers in Education.

Lujan, M.E., Stolworthy, D.L. and Wooden, S.L. (1986) *A Parent Training Early Intervention Program in Preschool Literacy*, ERIC Descriptive Report, ED 270 988.

Madriz, E.I. (1998) 'Using focus groups with lower socioeconomic status Latina women', *Qualitative Inquiry*, 24 (1): 114–28.

Manchester LEA (1988) *Early Literacy Project: a Framework for Assessment*. Manchester City Council Education Department.

McCormick, C.E. and Mason, J.M. (1986) 'Intervention procedures for increasing preschool children's interest in and knowledge about reading', in W. Teale and E. Sulzby (eds) *Emergent Literacy: writing and reading*. Norwood: Ablex Publishing Corporation.

McCracken, G. (1988). *The Long Interview*. Qualitative Research Methods 13. London: Sage.

McCulloch, G. (2001) *Doing Historical Research in Educational Settings*. Buckingham: Open University Press.

McCulloch, G. and Richardson, W. (2001) *Historical Research in Educational Settings*. Buckingham: Open University Press.

Merton, R.K. and Kendall, P.L. (1986) 'The focused interview', *American Journal of Sociology*, 51: 541–57.

Miles, M.B. and Huberman, A.M. (1994) *Qualitative Data Analysis: an Expanded Sourcebook*. London: Sage.

Mitchell, R.G. (1993) *Secrecy and Fieldwork*. Qualitative Research Methods 29. London: Sage.

Morgan, D.L. (1998) *Planning Focus Groups*. London: Sage.

Nfer-Nelson (1993) *LARR Test of Emergent Literacy: Teacher's Guide*. Windsor: Nfer.

Nutbrown, C. (ed.) (1996) *Respectful Educators: Capable Learners – Children's Rights and Early Education*. London: Paul Chapman/Sage.

Nutbrown, C. (1997) *Recognising Early Literacy Development: Assessing Children's Achievements*. London: Paul Chapman.

Nutbrown, C. (1998) 'Managing to include? Rights, responsibilities and respect', in P. Clough (ed.) *Managing Inclusive Education: From Policy to Experience*. London Paul Chapman/Sage.

Nutbrown, C. (1999) Focused Conservations in research. MA Study Unit Sheffield: University of Sheffield School of Education.

Nutbrown, C. (1999) 'Literacy in the Earliest Years: Alex's Story', in E. Millard (ed.) (1999) *Enquiring into Literacy*. Sheffield Papers in Education: University of Sheffield.

Nutbrown, C. (2001) 'Creating a palette of opportunities: situations of learning in the early years', in L. Abbott and C. Nutbrown, *Experiencing Reggio Emilia Implications for preschool*. Buckingham: Open University Press.

Nutbrown, C. and Hannon P. (eds) (1996) *Preparing for Early Literacy Development with Parents: a Professional Development Manual*. Nottingham/Sheffield: NES Arnold/The REAL Project.

Oakeshott, M. (1933) *Experience and its Modes*. Cambridge: Cambridge University Press.

Oakley, A. (1993), 'Interviewing women: a contradiction in terms', in H. Roberts (ed.), *Doing Feminist Research* (2nd ed.). London: Routledge.

Oliver, M. (2000) 'Profile', in P. Clough and J. Corbett *Theories of Inclusive Education: a Students' Guide*. London: Paul Chapman/Sage.

Parackal, M. (2001) 'Special educators in Beirut: a case study', in P. Clough and C. Nutbrown (eds), *Voices of Arabia: Essays in Educational Research*. Sheffield: University of Sheffield Papers in Education.

Perera, S. (2001) 'Living with "Special Educational Needs": mothers' perspectives', in P. Clough and C. Nutbrown (eds), *Voices of Arabia: Essays in Educational Research*. Sheffield: University of Sheffield Papers in Education.

Pink, S. (2001) *Doing Visual Ethnography: Images, Media and Representation in Research*. London: Sage.

Raymond, S. (2001) 'Excellent teaching: perceptions of Arab, Chinese and Canadian students', in P. Clough and C. Nutbrown (eds), *Voices of Arabia: Essays in Educational Research*. Sheffield: University of Sheffield Papers in Education.

Roffey, S. (2001) *Special Needs in the Early Years: Collaboration, Communication and Coordination* (2nd edn). London: David Fulton.

Rossman, G.B. and Rallis, S.F. (1998) *Learning in the Field: an Introduction to Qualitative Research*. London: Sage.

Rudestam, K.E. and Newton, R.R. (2001) *Surviving your Dissertation: a Comprehensive Guide to Content and Process* (2nd edn). Thousand Oaks: Sage.

Salmon, P. (1992) *Achieving a PhD: Ten Students' Experience* Stoke-on-Trent: Trentham Books.

Sebba, J. and Sachdev, D. (1997) *What Works in Inclusive Education*? Ilford: Barnardo's.

Segel, F. and Friedberg, J.B. (1991) 'Is today Liberry Day?' Community support for family literacy, *Language Arts*, 68: 654–657.

Seidman, I.E. (1991) *Interviewing as Qualitative Research – a Guide for Researchers in Education and the Social Sciences*. New York: Teachers College Press.

Shipman, M. (1981) 'Information through asking questions', in M. Shipman (ed.) *The Limitations of Social Research*. London: Longman.

Silverman, D. (2001) *Interpreting Qualitative Data: Methods for Analysing Talk, Text and Interaction* (2nd edn). London: Sage.

Stenhouse, L. (1975) An Introduction to Curriculum Research and Development. London: Heinemann.

Stewart, D.W. and Shamdasani, P.N. (1990). *Focus Groups: Theory and Practice*. Applied Social Research Methods Series 20. London: Sage.

Swarm, W. (1989) *Integration statistics: LEAs reveal local variations*, CSIE Factsheet. London: Centre for Studies on Integration in Education.

Swinson, J. (1985) A parental involvement project in a nursery school. *Educational Psychology in Practice*, 1: 19–22.

Thackray, D.V. and Thackray, L.E. (1974) *Thackray Reading Readiness Profiles*. London: Hodder and Stoughton.

Tierney, W.G. (1998) 'Life history's history: subjects foretold', *Qualitative Inquiry*, 4 (1): 49–70.

Toomey, D. and Sloane, J. (1994) 'Fostering children's early literacy development through parent involvement: a five-year program', in D.K. Dickinson (ed.) *Bridges to Literacy: children, families and schools*. Oxford: Blackwell Publishers.

Vaughn, K., Schumm, J.S. and Sunagub, J. (1996) *Focus Group Interviews in Education and Psychology*. London: Sage.

Vaughn, S., Shay, J., Schumm, J. and Sinagub, J. (1996) 'Focus group interviews – introduction', in S. Vaughn, J. Shay, J. Schumm and J. Sinagub *Focus Group Interviews in Education and Psychology*. London: Sage.

Vincent, D., Green, L., Francis, J. and Powney, J. (1983) *A review of reading tests*. London: National Foundation for Educational Research.

Vulliamy, G. and Webb, R. (eds) (1992) *Teacher Research and Special Educational Needs*. London: David Fulton.

Wade, B. (1984) *Story at home and school*. Educational Review Publication, 10 Birmingham: University of Birmingham, Faculty of Education.

Wade, B. and Moore, M. (1993) *Bookstart in Birmingham, Book Trust Report No 2*. London: Book Trust.

Walford, G. (ed.) (1991) *Doing Educational Research*. London: Routledge.

Walker, R. (1985) *Doing Research – a Handbook for Teachers*. London: Methuen.

Wandsworth Borough Council Education Department (1994) *Baseline Assessment Handbook*. London: Wandsworth LEA.

Waterland, L. (1989) *Apprenticeship in Action*. Stroud: Thimble Press.

Wedell, K. (1985) 'Future directions for research on children's special educational needs', *British Journal of Special Education*, 12 (1): 22–6.

Williams, R. (1965) *The Long Revolution*. Harmondsworth: Penguin.

Wilson, J. and Cowell, B. (1984) 'How shall we define handicap?' *British Journal of Special Education*, 1, (2): 33–5.

Winter, M. and Rouse, J. (1990) Fostering intergenerational literacy: the Missouri parents as teachers programme. *The Reading Teacher* 24: 382–386.

Wolfendale, S. (ed.) (2000) *Special Needs in the Early Years: Snapshots of Practice*. London: RoutledgeFalmer.

Ylisto, I. (1977). Early reading responses of young Finnish children. *Reading Teacher*, November: 167–172.

Index